Transcending Racial Divisions: Will You Stand by Me?

Transcending Racial Divisions: Will You Stand by Me?

Christine Louis-Dit-Sully

zer0
books

Winchester, UK
Washington, USA

JOHN HUNT PUBLISHING

First published by Zero Books, 2021
Zero Books is an imprint of John Hunt Publishing Ltd., No. 3 East St., Alresford,
Hampshire SO24 9EE, UK
office@jhpbooks.com
www.johnhuntpublishing.com
www.zero-books.net

For distributor details and how to order please visit the 'Ordering' section on our website.

ISBN: 978 1 78904 131 6
978 1 78904 132 3 (ebook)
Library of Congress Control Number: 2020937323

A CIP catalogue record for this book is available from the British Library.

Design: Stuart Davies

Printed and bound by CPI Group (UK) Ltd, Croydon, CR0 4YY

We operate a distinctive and ethical publishing philosophy in
all areas of our business, from our global network of authors to
production and worldwide distribution.

Contents

Acknowledgments

I would like to thank Ashley Frawley, Douglas Lain, Dominic James and others in John Hunt Publishing for giving me the great opportunity to express my views.

My thanks also to Dennis Hayes and Richard Ings for reading the earlier draft of my introduction and first chapter.

There are a few authors whose work and ideas have been invaluable to me over the years and some will be mentioned in this book. The British author Kenan Malik is the key author who greatly stimulated my thinking on the issue of race. Of course, this does not mean that he would necessarily agree with my interpretations and thoughts here.

This book has a single author but its main content is the result of the productive activity of two persons. Andreas Tintelott has been my silent but full partner since the beginning of this journey. A partnership with love and commitment is not a bartering contract or a loss of individuality as some would like us to believe today. I know how lucky I am to experience this loving partnership with Andreas.

To my dear parents, my dear siblings and others who have been with me, in good and bad, from day one.

Introduction

The issue of racism is both a personal and a political concern to me. I grew up with stories of my parents' hard lives in the French West Indies and of their living conditions when they arrived in mainland France in the early 1960s. I have also my own personal experiences growing up in France and spending part of my adult life in the UK. The issue of racism has never been far from my own personal life but it also became a political issue when I started to be involved with radical left-wing politics in the UK.

Until a couple of years ago, I was feeling that the problem of racism was getting much better. It seemed that, increasingly, most people did not simply see a black woman but actually saw me, a specific individual with my own good and bad sides. Imagine my consternation when I noticed that we seemed to be entering a time when, again, I was no longer an individual, a difficult person to deal with, a person who had loved scientific research and who is now realizing that her increasing passion for gardening may be an indication of her age. It seemed to me that I was again simply a black woman whose opinions and beliefs were apparently determined by her race and by others. The celebration of racial difference, previously encountered in the academic world, and the racialization of many issues seemed to have entered the public discussion with the help of current anti-racist activists.

Now, one of the initial disagreements I have had with some of the anti-racist activists was their use of personal experiences to argue that racism was everywhere and that it was getting worse. I started opposing them by pointing out that, in my personal experiences, this was not the case. We can rapidly see the problem with this. Our personal experiences are not enough to give us an objective idea of what is currently occurring in society.

My aim, when I started this book, was to challenge mainstream anti-racism promoted by proponents of left-wing/liberal/progressive/woke identity politics but from a point of view now known as that of the "radical old left." I do not believe that my personal experiences give me expertise. I am currently researching the issue and have decided it is time for me to actively enter the important conversation on race. This is also not a book where I argued that my personal experiences are better than others' personal experiences. Dismissing others because of their different backgrounds is neither right nor useful. I wanted to challenge some of the current ideas that are believed to be anti-racist today with the aim of advancing ideas that will help us confront racism, racial divisions and racial inequalities. I recognize that left and right no longer has real meaning in politics these days. Unfortunately, we do not yet have new words to replace them. What I mean by "radical old left" is a support for Marx's ideas and Enlightenment values which aim to challenge the status quo and radically transform society, its structures and institutions in order to promote progress and social equality. Social transformation, as it was understood in the past, was not simply about changing ourselves psychologically or changing our inner self to make us better individuals, but about finding new ways to organize society as a whole, in order for us to better live together. While I agree that different ethnic and racial groups face different social problems and barriers, I believe anti-racism based on politicized identities and identity politics is more of a hindrance than a solution. I certainly do not think, however, that we should forget about or ignore issues of racialization and racial discrimination and concentrate on the issue of class as some in the old left used to argue.

To illustrate just one of the reasons for my opposition to contemporary identity-based anti-racism, I had already written part of an introduction for this book where I was trying to highlight the fact that my mother, my sister and I are three black women, who have experienced racism, but do not have the same lives, the same opinions or the same world views, even though we are close and love each other dearly. I wanted to show that one of the reasons I oppose identity politics is because it imitates racist ideas in denying our individuality. It imposes the idea that, simply as a result of our common physical identities, I should feel a greater *political* solidarity with them than with humans with other physical characteristics but who may share my political opinions. To tell me that I cannot connect with, have empathy for or agree with someone else because they do not have the same identity or same personal experiences is like restraining me with one of those straightjackets that were once used for mental patients or prisoners. Identity politics is like a very narrow cage that prevents us from being our own selves, from developing our own thoughts and opinions, from making our own mistakes, from seeing, hearing, reading or discussing whatever ideas we want to, so that we can form our own opinions and try to reach a better understanding of the world and, hopefully, the truth. Grasping the truth is a difficult task for any of us but it is made impossible if we are restricted in our ability to think and discuss by those who think they are our betters, by those who think they can keep us in a very narrow lane. They are restricting our curiosity and our traveling path while we are attempting to cross a big, foreign field full of ideas begging to be discovered and understood. Yes, the crossing can certainly be dangerous. Yes, we can and do regularly fall down in this massive field of ideas, but who can tell us how much excitement or danger we should accept in our own life? This is our life. At the end of the day, the question about the type of society we want to live in is the kind of question that concerns us all, so most of us would want to enter that field together to find some answers and solutions. I agree with political theorist Hannah Arendt who believes that all humans are thinking beings who can reflect and judge if they want to. And she was right to argue:

Thinking actually undermines whatever there is of rigid rules, general opinions, and so forth. That is, there are no dangerous thoughts for the simple reason that thinking itself is such a dangerous enterprise. But I believe nonthinking is even more dangerous.[1]

Thinking can lead us to question some of our most important intellectual and moral foundations and consensuses. And thus, thinking is hard, painful and dangerous but it is essential.

Pervasive identity politics

While reading and thinking about the issues, I realized that many of those claiming to oppose identity politics also accepted some of the terrible ideas promoted by proponents of identity politics. The controversy over the caricature of the tennis player Serena Williams, drawn by the Australian cartoonist Mark Knight and published on 10 September 2018 in the *Herald Sun* newspaper, was a key turning-point in making me decide to change part of the focus of my book.[2]

I agreed with those who claimed that this was a racist caricature using the old racist stereotypes that used to be popular in our recent racist past. These racial stereotypes are based on the idea that you can describe any individual black person by just highlighting some features believed to be common to all black people. Racial stereotypes such as thick lips, a wide nose and dark brown skin were seen as sufficient to describe a black individual as if there were no distinct facial features that could distinguish one black person from another. She was drawn as a representative of a group, the angry black woman, rather than with her own specific facial features that would make us see her as an individual. Racism is about denying group members their individuality and that is why racial stereotypes and these kinds of drawings existed for groups of people who were oppressed, discriminated against or seen as inferiors, such as blacks, Jews

4

and Japanese.

The caricature of Serena Williams was racist and used specific well-known cultural tropes but this does not necessarily mean that the author was or is racist. I certainly did not support the hounding of and threats made toward the artist and his family, or the usual calls for censorship. I also do not believe that Serena Williams or any other black person should *not* be caricatured or be exempt from criticism of their behavior, opinions and claims to victimhood. However, supporting, as I do, the right to free speech, the right to criticize others for their behavior and the right to offend certainly does not mean ignoring (or even condoning) the racist content of a comment or criticism.

Some people's responses to the claim of racism with the cartoon are the reason I changed my mind about certain aspects of this book. I am very open about my strong opposition to identity politics and to the anti-white bigotry promoted by some black activists. I am also very open about my opposition to the current trend that sees constant claims of racism being made by people who racialize every aspect of our lives and see racism everywhere. I do not agree with the notion that white authors writing about black characters in their novels, plays, comics are necessarily being racist. I do not believe that having sexual preferences for people who are not dark-skinned themselves is inherently racist. I do not agree with the view that "blackface" is always racist. People have blackened and blacken their faces for various reasons including just for the fun of changing their appearance. I also find ridiculous and very unproductive the current fashion for trying to capture on camera someone hurling stupid racial insults, in the middle of an angry outburst. These little videos found all over the internet do not tell us anything about racism. Most of us would be lying if we tried to claim that we have never in our lives, when angry, hurled insults and made very stupid comments we very much regretted later. My husband would certainly call me a liar if I claimed this given that he has to live with my bad temper.

Despite this candor about my political views, acquaintances who know my opinions or even know me personally had no qualms about claiming that I was playing the race card when I argued that Serena's caricature was racist. This particular personal experience finally convinced me that my earlier suspicion was right. I think that the constant claims and accusations of racism by some proponents of identity politics have created a climate where any claim of racism is now seen as coming from easily offended people and can be safely dismissed by those opposing identity politics. This is a problem as we still live in a world where racism exists even if it is no longer the main social barrier for many who previously had experienced it in the West.

The most important point, however, is that identity politics has become so pervasive that its basic ideas and concepts are also accepted by their so-called opponents to justify their own opinions. My position that the caricature was racist was apparently due to me being a black woman. I could not possibly have thought about the issue and come to a rational conclusion. According to these so-called opponents of identity politics, I was playing the race card and becoming emotional because I am, like Serena Williams, a black woman. From this point of view, in this case, my identity as a black woman made the decision for me. Worse, if others could show me that other black people didn't agree with my opinion, then I would, apparently, realize my mistake. Somehow, sharing a skin color with them would mean I'd consider their opinions more informed and this would convince me. Part of racial thinking, which is one of the underlying ideas of identity politics, is to deny the moral and intellectual autonomy and individuality of members of a particular group of people. As seen here, the acceptance of racial thinking can be found among both the proponents of identity politics and their opponents. But we can only oppose racism if we also challenge racial thinking. If racism is only resisted by arguing that some races/ethnicities/cultures are not superior but that all are in fact equal, the result is only a challenge to the claim of superiority but not to the idea that we are from different, permanently divided groups. Only a universalist position can robustly oppose this damaging view that portrays humans as permanently divided. What a pessimistic view of the world and of us it is to think that we can never reach across our divisions to each other.

Looking at anti-racism and identity politics more closely, I also realized that it is no longer just a battle between those openly supporting identity politics and those opposing it. The fight is between groups of people who have divided the world into different, competing identities with each group claiming to support specific identities. For example: the working class was a particular social category, clearly analyzed by Karl Marx; it was defined by its particular social, economic and political position, with respect to the relations of production, in a specific historical period and in a specific social system we know as capitalism. Sociologists, however, have often defined it by the level of income, refusing to acknowledge the particular importance of the social relations of production in order to understand the world. This definition became adopted in mainstream discussions. Society, in sociology, became simply an aggregation of individuals differentiated by a level of income. Culture rather than race became a tool to distinguish social groups after World War 2 and the working class was defined by its own culture and traditions. Once people started to describe the working class as a matter of subjective self-identification, identifying it with a specific culture and traditions, it was not difficult to make the last step in portraying it as an identity group. The working class is now treated in essentialist and sociological ways, as an identity group with its own specific culture, morals, values and ways of life where one can be born into and never leave. Regardless of their current social position, academics, journalists, public intellectuals or members of government claim their identity as working class because they grew up in a working-class family. More importantly, the working class is increasingly defended using the language of victimhood the way identities are defined today, meaning the working class is now described as a group of victims. Victimhood claims today give moral authority when demanding resources from society. Portraying and defining members of a specific group as oppressors allows for acceptable moral condemnation and opposition to the groups' demands. Self-defined identity groups are based on real or imagined grievances, the members of that group are defined as victims and the identity is seen as positive. This is a very restricted vision of the world where one is defined either as oppressed or oppressor. Nevertheless, it is not surprising to hear a positive defense of this point of view answering that one can be both oppressed and oppressor. It reveals the current strength of this restricted vision.

Consequently, a once strong and well-organized collective group, the working class, originally described objectively is now a subjectively defined identity group with its members portrayed as oppressors by those wanting to demonize them or, by those defending them, as vulnerable victims, oppressed by their own political and social elites and/or suffering from an existential threat due to immigration.

Importance of debates

It is always sad to hear that there are people too emotionally exhausted to discuss important issues such as racism and anti-racism with others. Ironically, this claim of emotional exhaustion is now often made by black anti-racist activists themselves, i.e. by those who actually spend their time arguing about that very issue. It would seem that claims of emotional exhaustion have become a key aspect of drawing other people's pity and of being given a (very loud) voice in society, once again showing how the claim of victimhood today gives a perverse form of authority. Is that what anti-racist activists want now? To be pitied as poor emotionally exhausted black people? Regardless, this exhaustion is definitely not a valid reason for demanding that others do not criticize opinions and ideas. Claims of emotional exhaustion do not place a person beyond criticism, especially when discussing important political and social issues. In fact, one of the reasons I strongly challenge identity politics is down to my opposition to the belief that emotional exhaustion, skin color, race, ethnicity, culture or personal experiences automatically give one access to the truth and that that supposed truth cannot be discussed or challenged. My mother, my sister and I have different opinions about the issue of race and anti-racism. Which one of us has access to a truth that cannot be discussed or criticized?

In this book, I am trying to explain why current mainstream anti-racism in the context of a pervasive identity politics is not only unproductive and divisive but is leading us back to a darker age. I am hoping that this book will be seen as part of the conversation with the individuals interested in understanding the issue of race, in finding solutions to racial problems and being open-minded enough to read books that do not necessarily confirm their opinions and may even offend their opinions. I often complain to my husband or friends about books that really offend me. But I think the issue of racial divisions is just too important for us to restrict our reading to only a few opinions while ignoring all others or even worse, to demand that other opinions we do not like be censored. Everybody is complaining about tribalism these days but the main problem is the refusal to deal with ideas, the refusal to consider other people's ideas, to understand them and to challenge them if need be. Simply dismissing ideas has become a political pastime that will lead to nothing but permanent unproductive fighting. I think many of us are getting tired of these eternal fights that lead nowhere other than to an increasing collection of very creative or dull labels.

Past and present

I am arguing that anti-racism based on identity and identity politics is not challenging racism but is promoting racial thinking that used to be the domain of racists. The promotion of races as natural, permanent categories, the naturalization of difference, the promotion of victimhood status as a positive outcome one wants to achieve, the outlook that sees the world only through the prism of race is creating more divisions between people and more resentment. Anti-racism today has become a project to maintain the status quo but with a new minority of black people allowed to share in the wealth at the top. It hides behind terms such as "white supremacy," "white privilege" or "systemic racism," while the need to understand the current situation for different groups of people, discuss issues, develop new ideas and find new solutions is dismissed. Any inequalities or problems observed are automatically assumed to be down to racism thanks to the support for the deterministic explanation that all white people are racist, whether consciously or unconsciously. Essentially, the divisions between groups are described as insurmountable and permanent because, according to mainstream anti-racism, forces outside our control determine the opinions, ideas and attitudes of others.

Furthermore, I think that the current anti-racist movement and groups such as Black Lives Matter are not a continuation of glorious past struggles that demanded freedom, equal rights and equal treatment for all, visualizing a new world with equality for us all. These past struggles were still based on the Enlightenment's belief in the human capacity to reason, in the idea that we can all be considered as equally human and are all born equal, and in the ideal of universalism. The heroes of the past and the opposition they had to endure are continuously used to justify opinions and actions of present-day anti-racist

10

activists, and to claim moral authority over others, as if the big differences between the opinions and beliefs of the people of the past and those of today can be simply ignored or dismissed.

In fact, I also think that today's anti-racist groups based on identity politics are not even a continuation of the original 1960s social movements that started historically by promoting black pride, black power and black identity. They might have already given up on some of the Enlightenment ideas and were using an evolving concept of identity to carve out political space for themselves, but the promotion of victimhood, the portrayal of blacks as fragile beings needing protecting from words, attitudes or habits were certainly not parts of their identities. The cultural, social, political, economic and intellectual conditions these days are quite distinct from the conditions in the 1960s. The economic growth from the end of the Second World War till the early 1970s included a recovery period from the war followed by a period of counter-culture, youth culture and experimentation. Despite formal equal rights, these 1960-1970s fighters were still living in a very openly racist society. Traditional left-wing parties and trade unions were indifferent to their pleas. Isolated and disenchanted, some groups used the new concept of identity as a political tool of resistance. The black lesbian feminist group the Combahee River Collective seemed to have been the first to actually use the expression "identity politics" but they still had some sense of universalism in their politics.[3] They still demanded equal rights. Some people then considered that embracing their particular identity was temporary and that it would eventually help to destroy that identity later on, once they had achieved equal rights and equal treatment.

These are not the circumstances today. Contemporary groups and movements still use the concept of politicized identity but, based on dissimilar perceptions of the "individual," "society" and the "self," to portray themselves as victims and to demand recognition from those they see as enemies while still appealing to the state for protection. Present-day anti-racism is no longer a fight for freedom, civil liberties and autonomy, for the right to make our own decisions and control our own lives, but a demand for recognition and protection, a demand to keep things on the straight and narrow. It is no longer about transforming society and transcending racial divisions but about demanding that racial divisions be recognized and accepted as permanent and that the identity of those seen as vulnerable be protected by the political and social elites.

Racial ideology was not developed because of hate for the others but as a reaction to Enlightenment promises of equality. The reality of social inequalities, despite the claim to support Enlightenment ideals, had to be explained. The realities of social hierarchies, after the "death of God" and the promotion of reason and science, could no longer be explained as a God-given state of affairs. Natural biological interpretations were developed to explain away the gap between Enlightenment promises and social realities. Today, modern identity politics has the same role. The current focus with identity and the use of politicized identities follow a long tradition of deterministic explanations used to describe humans and to explain away social inequalities that still exist. The concept of race first developed as a biological category was then reinvented as a social construction or as a cultural category. Identity politics is based on the acceptance of these categories, going so far backward as even to reinclude biology despite racial science having been thoroughly discredited.

Highlighting the issue of racism as a problem of individual psychology and behavior, after the Second World War, has become really important for our political and cultural elites. It places blame for problems on those with less power and portrays the state and its institutions as the solution. It has also become a mechanism for distinguishing the elites as polite, civilized, educated and morally superior from the supposedly racist, xenophobic and uneducated ordinary people who need to be taught how to behave, how to think and how to vote. Mainstream anti-racism has become a tool of the authoritarian elites and self-appointed identity gatekeepers to maintain the status quo and to try and regain the legitimacy and authority they have lost, at the expense of ordinary people from all backgrounds.

If we really want to challenge racism and transcend racial divisions, we have to move away from racial thinking or any other kind of essentialist explanations that tell us we are completely determined by forces outside of our control, that we cannot change ourselves and the world and that we cannot control our own destiny. History shows us we are capable of changing ourselves, our morals, our own ideas and recognizing our shared interests against those desperate to keep their powerful position.

In Chapter 1, I will try to highlight how racial thinking, which developed the concept of race, is a product of history and as such is not immutable and fixed. I look briefly at the history of racial thinking and the context in which it was developed. This chapter challenges the current notions that racism is an original sin, part of white people's DNA or aspect of human nature. In Chapter 2, I will discuss another anti-political and deterministic explanation that followed the concept of biological race. The notion of culture has also played and is still playing a very important role in explaining social inequalities. Chapter 3 will address the various meanings of identity in the past and the present and the development of the modern identity politics used after the defeat of universalist radical politics. I will discuss the anti-political consequences of the politicization of social identities and will propose that the original development of identity politics started with the concepts of race, nation and culture and as a counter-Enlightenment reaction. There are past and modern notions of identity, which are dependent of distinct perceptions of the self, but the politicization of social identities started with the concept of race in the nineteenth century. In the conclusion, I briefly discuss the problem created by the concept of hate speech and the attack on freedom of speech. The principle of free speech has an essential role in any fight for freedom, including in the fight against racial thinking and racism. Future political action in order to transcend our racial divisions will need a public realm where we are free to engage and challenge all kinds of ideas in order to collectively develop a new universalist and political approach. Those of us hoping to create a better and freer world for all, those of us refusing to think that our concerns should only be limited to our private lives need to start trusting each other and build political solidarity, regardless of our races, ethnicities, cultures or nationalities.

One last note: I often use the word "black" with its past political meaning, not necessarily as a description for a specific race, skin color, ethnicity or identity. Black was a political term used for all those facing racialization, racial oppression and discrimination.

Chapter 1

Race is a Product of History

Racial thinking as dominant ideology in the West

Racial thinking, which is not the same as racism, is one of the dominant ideologies of the Western world. Interpreting the world, our human history and the social, political and philosophical issues as natural competition between different races is one of the most powerful trends in our current historical period. Whether race is seen as a biological category, a social category, a cultural category or a psychological category, racial thinking has become a fundamental prism through which the world is seen, understood, analyzed and interpreted. The idea of race is transformed into racism in practice when people think that others, who do not look the same as them, should be discriminated against, treated differently, hated or excluded. But the notion of race is also promoted by those celebrating differences between people, promoting racial identities, promoting the concept of diversity as a value and pushing for diversity policies in all areas of our lives.

We know that scientific and political critiques of racism did not necessarily mean a rejection of the idea of race as a biological concept. Those promoting racial equality, for example, can still believe in biological race but also think that all different biological races are equal. The notion of biological race was discredited after WW2 and the Holocaust and further discredited by substantial scientific evidence showing the hypothesis as false. It has, however, become attractive once more for those who think that science can give them the certainties missing from their lives. Rather than seeing science as a human method of enquiry based on reason, hypothesis, facts, collective human interpretations, evidence and analysis, some people see science as a worldview or a religion with dogmatic rules. As a consequence, they promote scientism, the idea that science can explain everything in our uncertain and scary human world.

I say that racial thinking has become a pervasive ideology but I definitely do not mean that we are all racist. The claim that we are all racist is constantly and wrongly made today. We are all, supposedly, contaminated by the ideas, education, habits and cultural traditions of white supremacy. We are all apparently racist, consciously and/or unconsciously. At heart, claiming that we are all racist is an easy way of justifying the beliefs that nothing can be done, it is human nature, part of the world we live in and everything is out of our control, except for desperate attempts in managing our permanent racism as best we can. This very pessimistic view of the world is one I certainly do not subscribe to and, in fact, strongly disagree with. Racial thinking is not a disease affecting human beings. Race is not "a condition. A disease. A card. A plague. Original sin," as Michael Eric Dyson enthusiastically claims before calling Robin DiAngelo "the new racial sheriff in town."[1] Promises of a cure, a prayer or a balm to make it bearable, supposedly developed by some enlightened individuals, are just empty words from those who have a very low opinion of us as gullible idiots, but who are still hoping to make money out of us. Anti-racism has, unfortunately, become a lucrative business these days and will attract individuals interested in money-making schemes. Again, I want to stress that applying racial thinking and seeing the world in terms of a supposed competition between different races does not necessarily equate to supporting racist ideas and racism. But the belief that humanity can be divided, using a few criteria, into distinct and permanent groups, and that members of these groups have specific mental and moral characteristics determining and explaining their social positions and social issues, is the basis that legitimizes our racial divisions.

Racial thinking before the modern concept
of racism

To understand the issue of racial thinking and its problems, we have to analyze separately the notion of race and the concept of racism. The concept of racism is much more recent than the concept of race. Apparently, "racism" first appeared in the title of a book written by Magnus Hirschfeld in 1933/34 who was challenging the notion of race hierarchy proposed by others in the nineteenth century, but he did not give a definition. The concept of racism was quickly taken up by others who were challenging the Nazi ideology of race.[2] Julian Huxley, Alfred Cort Haddon and Alexander Morris Carr-Saunders published in 1935 *We Europeans: A Survey of 'racial' Problems* where they provided a scientific critique of the Nazi theory of race by challenging scientific racism and racial science. This book was seen as an anti-racist statement and became popular. They, in fact, promoted what they thought was a better scientific understanding of race by arguing that races should be replaced with "ethnic groups" and "subspecies." The word "race," for them, had "lost any sharpness of meaning" and at their time of writing, had become "hardly definable in scientific terms."[3] They disagreed with the racial division of Jews by the Nazis, but still believed in the natural divisions of humanity into three biological groups.[4] Europeans could, in addition, be divided into three "minor sub species" (Nordic, Euroasiatic and Mediterranean) while the Aryan or Latin races could be termed "mixed ethnic groups."[5] Scientific and political critiques of racism, even though often opposing open expressions of racism, do not necessarily mean rejections of racial thinking. We see this also in the race equality discussions with those claiming that to "think as an antiracist" is to "think that racial groups are equal."[6] They may define racial groups using ancestry rather than simply skin color, but they are still promoting the concept of race.

Of course, racial theory which developed the concept of race is a necessary *a priori* condition before racism, racial prejudice and racial discrimination can develop. Thus, it is completely ahistorical or is an intent to rewrite history to talk about racist societies throughout human history when, for most of our history, the notion of race had not yet developed. According to American historian Ibram X. Kendi, a racist idea is "any concept that regards one racial group as inferior or superior to another racial group in any way."[7] Two important notions are in this definition: the notion of hierarchy and the notion of race. One cannot talk about a "racist idea" if there is not already a notion of "racial group" or "race," unless one is reading history backward and applying modern concepts to past understanding and beliefs. This notion only developed relatively recently so it is rewriting history to use the current notion of "black race," "white race" or "yellow race" and apply it to societies of the past that did not yet have this notion. The prejudices, in the past, toward strangers or people from other communities like African tribes, Slavs or Germanic tribes were not racial prejudices unless one imposes our current view of the world onto people long gone.

These days, in an attempt to highlight the suffering of a particular group of people, it has become common to rewrite history to try and extend the period of suffering far into the past. If they can show that a particular discrimination, a political or social situation has been happening for decades, centuries or even millennia, then they think it will add authority over their current demands for justice, privileges or protection. One of the problems with this is that they legitimize the notion of a linear or cyclical history with no sense of change and progress. They wrongly promote the belief that the past is the same as the present with, fundamentally, similar social, political, intellectual and economic circumstances, where human beings have not advanced by developing themselves and the society in which they live and where human actions and beliefs in the past can be interpreted in the same way as human actions and beliefs in the present or even in the future. This notion of history may be useful for those who want to promote themselves on the present-day hierarchy of suffering and oppression, but it also reflects as well as further entrenches the very pessimistic mood of Western society; a pessimism where any change is often seen as negative. There is a sense that everything is out of control or the result of the destructive nature of humanity, with no more beliefs in the potential of mankind to create a better society for themselves. The demands for change are more likely to be more regulations, policies and laws in order to control the mistrusted others. Portraying racism as a permanent feature of humanity, as the original sin or as an innate characteristic of a particular group or of humanity as a whole, reflects and contributes to this very pessimistic sentiment.

But, more importantly, we can also argue that viewing racism this way reflects the conservative aspect of some of the present-day anti-racism movement. The belief in a fixed human nature that determines our thoughts and beliefs or the conviction that race determines specific mental and moral characteristics are conservative ideas but so is the notion that history is simply a continuous line with no changes. As Frank Furedi noted: "For many conservative theorists history is the antithesis of historical thinking, understood as the attempt to grasp in thought the dynamic character of social development. For them history expresses not change, but continuity, the reproduction of old traditions in new circumstances."[8] Many of those who argue that racial thinking and racism have always existed do not try to understand the "dynamic character of social development" in order for us to comprehend the present and find solutions for the future but try to use their interpretation of the past in order to artificially create an identity such as the "black identity" for their own present purpose.

Racism is the political and social expression of the idea of

19

racial thinking whereby races are described as inferior or superior. These ideas are put into practice to organize society. The idea of race and notion of hierarchy in races should be strongly opposed but not by simply challenging the notion of "hierarchy" itself. Making a judgment that a group is superior or inferior over another group using specific criteria is not wrong in itself. We do appreciate and discuss whether a specific sports team is technically superior to another team. The notion of racial hierarchy is a problem because it is based on a social order described as racial order to make it natural, permanent but more importantly legitimate. Using biology and science, social inequality became racial inequality in the nineteenth century, first when describing social groups such as the lower and upper classes within European societies and then when discussing differences between European societies, their colonies and the rest of the world.

Racial thinking, not a permanent and natural aspect of our lives

Despite the present-day pervasiveness of racial thinking, it does not mean it was an inevitable development in human philosophy and ideas nor does it mean that racial thinking and the concept of race have always existed. The concept of race did not arrive naturally and fully formed, was not invented by some hateful people and is not the product of a human predilection for hate. In fact, it did not exist for most of our human history and this fact alone tells us that it is possible to think in other ways. It is also not an accidental development, meaning that it did not just develop out of nowhere but is an historical development, a concept which developed within specific historical, intellectual, social and economic circumstances. Race today became a reality, although not a *biological* reality, through the struggles of humanity. Different groups of human beings fought each other as well as struggling against nature and other external forces, within a developing social organization known as capitalism. Both the social circumstances and the struggles throughout history change, and so does the meaning of race. Race is a product of history.

I think it is important to understand how racial thinking developed and why race became such an important feature of our lives, because it can allow us to find alternative ways of thinking about ourselves and alternative ways of organizing our society. Understanding how and why the concept of race was developed might help us move away from this concept and the resulting problems racism has created for many people over the last few centuries. Of course, my argument is based on the currently uncommon assumption and belief that humanity can control its destiny and that we are not just the product of our psychology which supposedly makes us hate others and forces us to remain racially separated. Many of us, in the twenty-first century, do not hate others because of their skin color or ancestry and many of us actually think it immoral to discriminate against them because of their supposed membership of a particular race. Is the psychology of those of us who think this way not human too, or do we simply have different political and moral opinions which oppose racism? The fact that our attitudes toward others have changed over the course of history on many issues such as identity, intermarriage, nationalism, the place of God in society and so on suggests that racial thinking or racist attitudes are no more permanent features determined by our human psychology than any other issue. Political, philosophical and moral opinions have been discussed, promoted, challenged, developed and changed throughout history. For example, a follow-up of a 2012 study claims that today 90 percent of people in England do not believe you have to be white to be considered English and that the biggest shift from 2012 was within the older generation, the over-65s. Apparently, in 2012, 35 percent of them believed that ethnicity was a determining factor for Englishness but, in

2019, only 16 percent still believed this.[9] Of course, we have to be careful with surveys like this. People have a tendency not to reveal unpopular views, but even the fact that associating Englishness with whiteness is seen as unpopular today shows how moral and political opinions can change over time. Racial thinking and racism can be challenged.

In fact, when one looks at the meaning of race throughout our history, one can clearly see that race is a product of historical and social development. The roots of racial thinking are found in the eighteenth century although like any other ideas and concepts, their development did not follow a straightforward linear path. Many ideas, in different social contexts, were discussed, accepted, discarded or developed on the way to the current meaning of race. Certain ideas may become popular at a particular historical time if they express the contemporary interests of social forces such as those of the ruling class, the working class, women or young people but may become rejected later. But the more specific and important point here is that the existence or absence of racial theories in various societies reflects specific historical and social views of the relationship between humanity, society and nature.[10] Our understanding of this relationship has changed throughout our history and social development. The philosophers in antiquity, for example, who did not develop racial theories, did not understand this relationship the way we do today.

Recognizing human diversity, not race

People in antiquity did not perceive each other through the concept of race. Of course, like all of humanity, they saw physical differences between groups of people and the Greeks considered themselves superior to others but recognizing differences between humans is not the same as arguing for specific and distinct races. Acknowledging the existence of human variation does not mean grouping humanity into distinct and immutable groups, with specific biological characteristics seen as significant and important in determining cultural characteristics. There are two ways to view these variations. Human variation, physical and cultural, can be seen as the result of differences in degree or differences in kind. Racial thinking creates divisions in kind and states that these divisions determine the behavior and mental abilities of specific groups. In ancient Greece, environmental factors such as geography and climate were thought to be the cause of human physical diversity. This implied that changing the environment would lead to changes in observed differences. They did not see the character of individuals, their social status or the structural organization of communities as permanent features based on the physical differences between groups of humans. Their interactions with other groups were not determined by differences in phenotypes but by the fact they were from different communities, from different familial or tribal affiliations. The Greeks saw themselves as superior mainly because they had developed a political society with new ways of thinking while others were seen as still living within a natural/ primitive society. The ancient Greeks had invented political theory. They wanted to use critical reason to systematically analyze and question "the very foundations and legitimacy of traditional moral rules and the principles of political right."[11] They had developed a civic community, a community of citizens divided, not by race, but by classes such as peasants, landlords or artisans, where political conflicts could be resolved. This civic community was also not a master/servant or ruler/subject community as seen elsewhere. While building their sophisticated political and democratic society, the traditional notions of families, clans, birth, blood or household were progressively replaced by the notion of citizenship.[12] As Ivan Hannaford has argued in his book *Race: The History of an Idea in the West*, the ancient Greeks' concepts of "politics" and "citizenship" were a barrier to the development of the concept of biological race within their society. Seeing race as an antonym to politics, a thought suggested by Michael Oakeshott to Hannaford[13], is an important idea to pursue; I think it gives us a key to finding a solution to some of our current social and political problems. If our racial identity is more important than our membership of a community of citizens, then we are ruled by an out-of-our-control nature rather than by a man-made political and moral world.

In ancient Greece, individuals were judged according to whether or not they were part of a "public arena." Citizens, the only individuals involved in the public world, were the ones participating in the important discussions and decisions concerning the future of their society. Their role was not simply to uphold the customs and habits determined by their ancestors as if they were just gatekeepers for traditions and culture, but also to discuss contemporary problems and make decisions about how to deal with them. The new form of governance, "democracy," that they developed had firm restrictions on who could be a citizen (no women or slaves) but their society was based on the concepts of "the civic" and "the political," not "the racial."

Greek citizens were involved both in the domestic world and the public world. The domestic world, one that nobody could fully escape from, formed by the household and the family was the only place women and slaves could "live." This world was seen as subject to the rules of nature (*physis*), kinship, hierarchy and inequality. More importantly, being chained to the domestic sphere alone, as women were, was seen as living a purposeless existence ruled only by the laws of nature. The public arena, available only to citizens, was seen as subject to the rules of man-made laws (*nomos*). Even though there was a constant struggle between the lower classes and high classes, citizens of all classes were seen as equal politically and all with the right and duty to participate in decisions for the common good of society. Those in the public sphere were seen as having a purpose in life. For the Greeks, communities which did not have politics but were only regulated by customs and habits were seen as primitive living only according to the rules of the natural world. Aristotle believed that the polis, the Greek city-state and the community of citizens, was the best way to organize society in order to achieve the good life.

According to Frank M Snowden, Jr, a well-known scholar on black people in classical antiquity, "natural bent, not race, determines nobility" for the ancient Greeks. He argued that racial prejudice in ancient Rome and ancient Greece was not an issue.[14] Although they made a distinction between Greeks and non-Greeks, individuals were judged by their own character, quality and excellence in living the good life, not by their racial purity. For the ancient Greeks, the people from northern countries were simply known as "Scythians" while those coming from the South were labeled as "Ethiopians." The observed human variation was explained in the same ways for all groups of people with no notion of superiority and inferiority due to skin color. More importantly, no negative attitude and no laws existed prohibiting miscegenation or racial mixing between "Ethiopians" and "Mediterranean whites."[15]

I am discussing the ancient Greeks not as a call for us to go back to their way of life, but to highlight the fact that there are other ways of thinking outside our current racial theory. For racial thinking to develop later, new ways of comprehending the relationship between individuals, society and nature had to be cultivated. The understanding of this relationship has changed throughout our history, as just illustrated here with the difference between our modern world and the Ancient World. The historical conditions that allowed the development of political theory in ancient Greece had to have included a belief in human agency, in humanity's role in determining its own destiny. We live in a modern world where nature has much less influence on us than on people in antiquity, where we have developed, for example, medical, scientific and technological tools to help us free ourselves from nature constraints/domination and yet, the belief in humanity's ability to control its destiny is rare. We currently have a very low expectation of what humans can achieve. The environment, races, cultures, biology, nationalities, sex are constantly seen as factors determining individuals and communities' behavior and characters, giving little role or no room for humanity's actions. Environmentalism, racialism, nationalism, conservatism, individualism, communism, religions or identity politics, for example, all have their own specific understanding of what it means to be human and a particular grasp of the relationships between an individual, the community/collective/society and the natural world. Kenan Malik noted that like "Plato, Aristotle saw the needs of the individual as subordinate to those of the collective" and, as seen with our modern discussions on subjects such as climate change, capitalism or neoliberalism, humanity is still actively debating whether this is the right approach.[16]

The divisions, the barbarism, the cruelty and the slavery of the Ancient World were not based on the concept of race but on whether people were seen as part of the public arena, the domestic arena or from other societies with no politics. Slavery in the Greco-Roman world, and for most of our history, was based on the notion of "Might is Right," meaning that the most powerful people can conquer others and do what they want with the conquered. What is right is determined by the most powerful people. This leads to another important point about the history of racial thinking. Previously, the "might is right" theory was justification for the acts of many communities in the world, including in Europe. The "might is right" theory is a doctrine which asserts that the superiority of the conquerors over the conquered is due to the historical fact of conquest, of having shown physical strength over the conquered. Superiority was seen as being a result of historical events such as winning a war, or a greater ability to use force over others, not because of theorized physical superiority. Natural strength can help win a war, but so can a specific military culture or a well-organized society. However, it was the victory itself that led to the claim that a community was superior to another. Racial theory introduced the idea that the speculated physical and psychological abilities of a particular community shapes and predicts the superiority or inferiority of a community.

God and Race

For the idea of race to finally develop, the classical Greco-Roman political view of members of society, and the Judeo-Christian religious view of the faith community had to be replaced by a new and purely biological vision of "natural Man." Before the biological view of the world appeared in Western thought, the Jewish and Muslim religions had already colonized much of the political world, changing it and damaging it.[17] These two religions promoted the idea that there was a direct relationship between Man and God and that the laws which needed to be obeyed are those revealed by God, not man made. Worshiping God and observing religious rules in daily life was seen as being at the center of human existence. "Citizenship" was no longer a consequence of the ability to reason philosophically and politically in a Greek or Roman public arena but the result of membership of the Jewish or Christian faith community. For example, the Church developed arguments to justify its involvement in political affairs, its role in providing important moral guidance to the rulers of man's world. Essentially, the Church not only involved itself in God's affairs and in the saving of men's souls but also had a certain hold over human affairs on Earth. Earlier Christian rulers had to answer to Rome for example.

Prior to the Enlightenment's attack on religion and tradition and the rise of the idea of understanding the world through reason, Europeans generally saw the human world as divided between Christians, Jews, Muslims and "heathens." The new notion of the "biological natural human" replacing the notion of the "child of God" provided the space for the concept of the biological race. In the Christian world, the previous belief that the common ancestor of all human beings was Adam had not left much room for the potential picture which describes people as belonging to different races from distinct ancestors. The Enlightenment's critique of religion and tradition and the triumph of the scientific revolution helped in giving space for the potential development of the concept of biological race.

Pre-racial ideas

It is possible to argue that the first pre-racial ideas appeared with the Spanish "blood purity" (limpieza de sangre) laws and the expulsion of the Jews in 1492 and of the Muslims a decade later. But then again, Spanish laws made use of the Jewish notion of purity of blood which was not a biological notion but a religious, genealogical one. The Spanish argued that they wanted to preserve the purity of Christian lineage, and thus discriminated against or expelled anybody with Jewish, Muslim or heretical ancestry.[18] This "purity of blood" concept also became important in the context of the Spanish colonial adventures in South America.

Throughout the sixteenth century, the Spanish argued that South American natives were not necessarily impure of blood until they had rejected Christianity, and that the role of Spain was to bring these people into the membership of the Christian faith. Nonetheless, there were also discussions about the nature of the native population who were very badly treated and often forced to become slaves. Were they humans or an inferior species? Bartolomé de Las Casas became a fierce opponent of slavery and ill-treatment in South America. He initially owned slaves himself but after entering the priesthood, he argued that South American natives were humans. For the rest of his life, he fought against the unjust treatment they received from the Spanish.[19] The arguments used by Las Casas and the resulting proclamation by Pope Paul III, in 1537, opposing the enslavement of native South Americans are thought to be quite important in the history of the idea of race, morality and politics. Las Casas argued that the natives of the New World were true humans possessing reason and were thus capable of being part of the Christian faith and being equal citizens under the law. These qualities, Las Casas argued, meant it would be heretical to take their property and their political liberty from them and to enslave them.[20]

What is even more historically important is the Valladolid debate, on July 8, 1550. It is considered to be the first European moral debate on the treatment of colonized people by colonizers. Las Casas argued that Aristotle's point stating that some people may be by nature slaves is not a justification for the claim of natural superiority of one group over another, especially in this case, where the natives possess reason. He essentially highlighted the difference between the natural and political worlds and argued that the contemporary barbaric customs of native South Americans such as human sacrifice did not prevent them from entering the Christian faith later because they also had reason.[21] In essence, Spain in the sixteenth century was concerned about the rights and treatment of colonized people, long before this important moral discussion was ever considered in other European countries. That is not to say that cruelty, persecution and enslavement did not occur in colonial South America after the banning of slavery regarding native South Americans. Natives still suffered all of these. And it is worth noting that the Spanish had not prohibited the enslavement of Africans who became a significant section of the population in colonial South America.

From the sixteenth century onwards, Europeans, in great numbers and with a willingness to take great risks with their own lives and wealth, set sail to explore the largely unknown world. Curiosity about the world and people living in it, a sense of adventure and of wonder, a need to search for material benefits, but also a search for the "noble savage" were characteristics which drove them to travel. Writing about journeys and experiences of traveling became an important part of Western literature between the sixteenth and eighteenth centuries with a rising interest in exoticism and primitivism. The rapid social changes that occurred with first the scientific revolution but later with the industrial revolution and development of capitalism overthrowing the old social systems, also led to increased nostalgia about the past and the traditions. Curiosity about and interest in the "bon sauvage" (noble savage) and his traditions was, in reality, an idealization and romanticization of those seen as primitive peoples still living close to nature. The way of life of the "noble savage" was contrasted with the Western way of life, seen by some as becoming increasingly complex and superficial. Primitivism originates more from criticism and/or rejection of one's own society than knowledge and appreciation of other communities. As Todorov noted, the more poles apart a particular community or culture is from one's own, the better candidate for idealization. With the idea of the noble savage living nearer to nature, the past Western society, seen also as nearer to nature, could be recreated and celebrated.[22]

During the "long eighteenth century" of the Enlightenment period (end of the seventeenth century till the beginning of the nineteenth century), intellectuals and philosophers favored the rejection of religion, old beliefs and traditions and promoted the importance of reason, experimentations and observations in order to understand the world but more specifically to understand human nature. Enlightenment philosophers attempted to "overturn every intellectual assumption, every dogma, every "prejudice" (a favorite term) that had previously exercised any hold over the minds of men."[23] The concern of the Enlightenment which should be seen as an open-ended process was an attempt to understand human nature and humanity's past in order to predict humanity's future and its social development. The belief in a universal human nature and rejection of the divine led to the need to describe humanity in all of its characteristics such as its passions, its sociability and its place in nature. Studying the differences and similarities between different communities and imitating aspects of the natural sciences became an important part of the new human science.[24] One of the roots of racial thinking was an intellectual search to understand a universal and fixed human nature. The original motivation was not an innate hatred of the others. But then, the racial discourse was further expanded to explain class differences in European societies before a more developed concept of race was applied to explain differences between Europeans and the rest of the world.

Natural history and Race

In 1684, Francois Bernier, a French physician and traveler, published his work translated as, "A new division of the Earth according to the different species or races which inhabit it," and considered to be the first classification of humanity into different races. Rather than use the old divisions into Christians, Muslims, Jews and heathens, Bernier argued that geographers should not divide "the world only according to the different countries or regions" but use a classification based on different observable human characteristics. He described humans as if they could be divided into four different racial groups: Europeans, Far Easterners, Negroes and Lapps. Lapps were the only group he described negatively.[25] He thought that the differences he observed were partly due to the environment in which people lived.

In the early discussions of race, the search for historical and biological human origins started an important debate between monogenists, who argued for a single origin of all human races, and polygenists, who argued that different races had different origins. The natural historians' main interests in collecting, describing and classifying humans and the belief in equality promoted by some of the philosophers of the Enlightenment meant that the new racial discussions were not as focused on the idea of innate superiority and inferiority as what is found in later discussions. More significantly, the belief in human perfectibility and in the possibility for human universalism promoted by Enlightenment philosophers, in the eighteenth century, were still obstacles to the idea of racial hierarchy where some races are seen as permanently and inherently uncivilized. In the eighteenth century, Carl Linnaeus, a Swedish naturalist and a devout Christian, Professor of Botany and the father of taxonomy (the system of classifying and naming organisms) devoted his life to trying to discover the natural order of God's creation by studying plants and animals. He believed humans were one species and named the species *Homo sapiens* but divided the species into five groups; *Europaeus albus* ("white European"), *Americanus rubescus* ("red American"), *Asiaticus luridus* ("yellow Asiatic"), *Afer niger* ("black Negro") and *Homo ferus* ("wild, cruel, savage man").[26]

A contemporary of Linnaeus and a very influential authority in natural history, George Louis Leclerc, Comte de Buffon, insisted on human unity and on the differences and superiority of mankind over animals. It was not because of Christian beliefs that he agreed with a single species but because he reasoned, as a naturalist, that the fact that blacks and whites can have children together proved they belonged to a single species. Reason was the criterion he used to establish human superiority over animals. "Man is a reasoning being; the animal is totally deprived of that noble faculty" he argued, and all varieties of Man had reason and language: "The savage and the civilized man have the same powers of utterance; both speak naturally, and are equally understood."[27] According to Buffon, the different varieties of humans observed were a result of the temperature, altitude, diet and social customs. He thought that later generations of black people living in a colder climate would have whiter skin. Human unity also implied that all humans can be judged by the same standards and that a hierarchy within the species could be described by analyzing specific characteristics such as the sociability of communities. The smaller communities were the less sociable and so the less socially developed. The nations of Western Europe were deemed at the top of the hierarchy while the small Native Americans were at the bottom. White Europeans were the norm in order to compare all other groups: "Nature, in her most perfect exertions, made men white,"[28] and thus blacks' inferiority was enough reason for them to be subjugated and reduced to slavery.

Buffon's scientific reputation allowed him to promote his racialist ideas which link the physical characteristics such as skin color and body size with specific levels of civilization, culture and morality. Still, an important point to stress here is that despite Buffon's early racialist opinions, the word "race" was rarely used before the nineteenth century. Earlier descriptions of human diversity and attempts to understand differences between people were not comparable to nineteenth-century discussions of race. There was still no belief that humans could be permanently separated, with the help of biology, into distinct and self-reproducing groups. Buffon, for example, still believed the observed differences, including physical differences, were due to the environment and culture. This led him to think that education could eventually change people, even though it might take years.

The issue of chattel slavery in the United States and the original egalitarian sentiment behind the American claim to independence had, of course, influences on the discourse of race. The case of Thomas Jefferson highlights the tensions and contradictions found in individuals' beliefs and opinions. These contradictions and tensions are found also between abstract beliefs and principles supported by people and the reality of social life and practice. Thomas Jefferson was part of the social and political movement which tried to apply some of the Enlightenment ideals to create a new society out of the old feudal regime. The new and developing capitalist forces and social relations of production did destroy some of the old divisions such as the division between the king and his subjects. But the new divisions between the new capitalists and the emerging working class or the old divisions between the laboring classes, slaves and plantation owners came to be seen as permanent and natural. Thomas Jefferson was a Founding Father of the United States and principal author of the US Declaration of Independence that states that "all men are created equal." Still, he believed that the mental and moral characteristics of people of African descent, such as their perceived lack of imagination, proved their inferiority.[29] In his *"Notes on the State of Virginia"* he raised his suspicion "that the blacks, whether originally a distinct race, or made distinct by time and circumstances, are inferior to the whites in the endowments both of body and mind." Apparently, his personal observations led him to believe that blacks and whites could not live free together. And he attempted to rationalize it, even though he disagreed with most natural historians of his time. Mostly opposed to slavery, he still raised his suspicions that the "unfortunate difference of color, and perhaps of faculty, is a powerful obstacle to the emancipation of these people."[30] Jefferson's contradictions and reasoning could also be seen as a journey from the hope of seeing social equality, to observing constant inequality even in the new society to finally concluding that some people can never be equal.

Johann Friedrich Blumenbach, Professor of Medicine in Germany, is considered the father of craniology and, together with Buffon, the founder of anthropology. He also believed in the unity of the human species but thought that mankind could be divided into five varieties, some of which are still frequently used today: Caucasian, Mongolian, Ethiopian, American and Malay.[31] However, it is important to notice here that he did not think these varieties were fixed and immutable. The climate, environment, mode of life and other factors were thought to be responsible for the variations in humanity. He was opposed to the idea of superiority and inferiority between varieties of humans but, contrary to many today, he attacked those who did not separate humans, possessor of speech and reason, from the orangutan. Interestingly, these early theories of human variety on the monogenist side were seen as potential theories able to replace the medieval European notion, based on the Hebrew book of Genesis, which states that humanity is under one God and divided into three groups, the descendants of Noah's three sons. The three sons had survived the flood with Noah in the Ark: Shem fathered the Semitic people including the Jews; his offspring inherited the Promised Land and populated the Indian Ocean, Persia and Armenia. Japheth's offspring populated Europe; while Ham's offspring populated Africa, Egypt and Libya. Ham's descendants were cursed by Noah while Shem's and Japheth's were blessed; Ham was accused of laughing at his sleeping father's naked body while his two brothers covered it up.

Although polygenism became a more popular theory only in the nineteenth-century discussions of race, in the previous century Voltaire and Lord Kames had been two advocates of the idea of separate species of humans. Polygenism was associated with a radical anti-religious outlook and with blasphemy. Trying to explain the differences between Africans and Europeans, Voltaire (François-Marie Arouet), French writer, historian and philosopher, declared that, "it is not improbable that in warm climates apes have ravished girls."[32] He thought

Native Americans and blacks were distinct species from Europeans not just because of the differences in their physical appearances but also because of their levels of civilization and intelligence. Nonetheless, he still recognized rationality and sociability as common characteristics of all species of humans. As we can see, Voltaire was an Enlightenment thinker who did not really believe in equality. Enlightenment was certainly not one coherent homogenous movement where all philosophers and intellectuals supported the same ideas. Henry Home, Lord Kames, the Scottish jurist and philosopher, is another example of an intellectual who, involved in the discussion of the nature of human species, attempted to use scientific reasoning to justify his political opinions. He used examples of interbreeding and fertile offspring found in the animal kingdom, such as that between hares and rabbits, to argue that the possibility of having fertile children produced by mixed couples of blacks and white Europeans did not gainsay the idea that blacks and whites were also two different species.[33]

Thus, in the eighteenth century, the main explanations for the differences between people were still the ideas describing a causal effect on people by the natural and/or social environment such as climate or culture. There was still no coherent theory of race, and human history was still not seen as a history of a competition between races. It is worth observing here that most of these past ideas expressed by these intellectuals are seen as shocking today by most people. The difference, between the past and the present, in the way we accept or reject these ideas is the result of humanity's social, moral and intellectual progress.

Development of the concept of race against Enlightenment's universalism and equality

In the nineteenth century, the egalitarian and universalistic attitude of the Enlightenment had less and less influence on the discourse of race. The second half of the nineteenth century saw the development of what is now known as "scientific racism," the racial theory that explains human differences by grouping people into distinct and immutable biological units. The progress in biological sciences was used to promote the idea that people can be biologically separated into discrete and distinct groups and that each of these biological groups have their own physical, cultural and mental abilities. Biological races have been discredited in the twentieth century, even though some sections of society, supporting scientism, are currently trying to revive this by arguing that science answers all questions. What we will see later is that biological races may have been discredited but the perception that humans can be divided into immutable and distinct groups was not questioned. The concept of "ethnic group" and "culture" replaced the concept of biological race. Identities, in the twenty-first century, have become another way of understanding the relationship between humanity, society and nature where immutable differences are used to explain social relations and human interactions.

At the beginning of the nineteenth century, the debate between those who believed in a single human species and those who argued that races were groups of people with entirely different ancestors from other groups was still very much alive until Darwin's theory of evolution. Strong support for the monogenist argument came from James Cowles Prichard, an English anthropologist and ethnologist, who is considered the founder of English anthropology. He argued that all variants of the human being had the same inner nature. According to him, the human race was originally black and lighter skin came later, once civilization had developed.[34] In the United States of America, the leader of the polygenist side was Dr Samuel George Morton, a very famous physician and researcher in natural history, who argued that the single Creation story claimed by the Bible was wrong. He suggested that studying human cranial capacity and "mixed-race" people would help in determining the origin of the different races as well as determining their mental ability. His conclusions? Native Americans were "averse to cultivation, and slow in acquiring knowledge; restless, revengeful, and fond of war, and wholly destitute of maritime adventure" while blacks were "joyous, flexible, and indolent" and constituted the "lowest grade of humanity."[35] He was famous for personally collecting more than a thousand human skulls, determined as he was in showing a relationship between the size of a skull and a biological race.[36] Louis Agassiz, a Swiss naturalist, became a supporter of the polygenist side after seeing black people when he moved to the United States. Their anatomical differences convinced him that they could not be the same species as the "White man." Interestingly, Agassiz's and Morton's polygenism was challenged by John Bachman, the minister of St John's Lutheran Church in Charleston, South Carolina who believed in the common origin of the human species, despite his commitment to slavery. As we saw before, the polygenist argument was seen as anti-Christian, thus, defenders of slavery were not always keen in using this idea to support their notion of superiority and inferiority between races. Using the story of Shem, Ham and Japheth, Bachman argued that the fact that people of African descent were part of the human race did not mean they were not inferior to white Europeans. Blacks are "still everywhere the servants of servants" he declared.[37]

In France, the question of the unity of the human race or of the different origins of the human types became very contentious during the first half of the nineteenth century. Jean Baptiste Lamarck, a French naturalist, who was one of the first to use the word "biology," to describe the new science aiming to understand the "origin and development of living organisms"[38], had argued that all species, including the human species, were not fixed and that the environment had an impact on all living organisms. He was the first to develop a coherent theory of evolution elaborating on his idea that species transform into other species. His ambitious aim was to understand the chronological order of the birth of all living organisms.[39] French naturalist Etienne Geoffroy Saint-Hilaire supported his position on evolution but he faced strong opposition from the rest of the scientific community who resisted the idea of evolution for living organisms. For some people, his theory was still too radical against religious beliefs. One of his main opponents was eminent paleontologist and zoologist Georges Cuvier who established the notion of species extinction as a scientific fact. He made the case for the fixity of species and argued that changes in a species would lead to its disappearance, making evolution of species unlikely. Thus, the differences in human types could not be due to evolution and change if one rejects Lamarck's theory but from having different ancestry if Cuvier's position is preferred.

The dispute influenced and was influenced by the theory of evolution discussed after Charles Darwin's publication of the *Origin of the Species* in 1859. Darwin's theory of evolution curtailed the monogenist-polygenist debate given that not only the human species but all species were now thought to come from a single ancestor. But the theory of evolution led the development of racial theory in a new direction where different human races were explained as inferior or superior according to their degree of evolution between the ape and the higher evolved types of humans. I think some of us old enough can still remember the "closest to the ape" insult thrown at black people in the past. The confirmation of the single origin of the human species did not challenge the idea that there were different biological races, nor did it challenge the idea of a hierarchy between races. Darwin's theory did, however, pose a challenge to numerous other discussions around race, such as the influence of geography and climate on skin color or body shape.

Political and social concerns led the progress in racial thinking. Scientific explanations followed, adapted and were used to respond to these concerns. There were many European and American intellectuals involved in the discussion of race and my intention is not to give detailed information about these discussions or even a brief overview which would still most likely involve a few hundred pages. I just want to provide a glimpse into the complex intellectual origins of racial thinking. The contemporary reduction of this history by some people to an extremely simplistic "white people hate black people" in no way helps us to understand the issue of race in the past and present.

The idea of race became fully formed in the second half of the nineteenth century, after the American and French Revolutions and the important social troubles throughout Europe that followed these revolutions. By the mid-nineteenth century, anthropologists, among others, started to assert that humans could be divided into distinct races. They argued that these categories were natural, immutable and objective and that each race had its own specific cultural development, culture and way of life. They promoted the idea that social phenomena such as poverty or culture were biologically determined. Defining races by characteristics such as skin color, facial appearance, hair texture and color, and cranial profile, they argued that membership of a specific race would predetermine individual and group behavior, intelligence and moral character. It is clear that the concept of race was first developed within the European and American intellectual community before it became widely accepted in society. But the point to stress is that we cannot understand the growth of racial thinking without understanding the relationship between the intellectual discussions and the social, economic and political contexts in which these concerns and intellectual discussions arose. This is true both for the development of racial thought in the past and for the contemporary racial thinking and racist ideas.

Again, and again, people promote the belief that racial and racist ideas come only from inarticulate, uninformed, non-educated, rough, loud, idiotic, illogical individuals who have no evidence for their hatred and bigotry. A simple look at the history of racial thought could easily dispel this belief. Intellectuals, scientists, government officials and members of the upper classes developed and/or promoted racial theories and racist ideas down to the rest of the population. They eventually became accepted by the public because they seem to interpret the world and people's experiences correctly and because there were no strong alternative interpretations.

Again today, academics and intellectuals throwing around statistics and "evidence" are celebrated for being rational, thoughtful and speaking well while the racist and/or xenophobic content of their speech is ignored or unchallenged by all sides. Some involved in left-wing politics, who only throw labels like "racist," "bigot," "xenophobic" or "Nazi" at people, do not oppose the specific ideas and interpretations promoted but show a painful lack of counter-arguments against the racist and xenophobic content of intellectuals' and academics' speech. Another section of society, often claiming to oppose the identitarian left, and often admiring "these rational and articulate academics who are very unlike the hysterical, loud and censorious woke left," ironically show the same attitude as those they criticize. They completely ignore the content of speech, refuse to engage with the ideas and leave the racist and xenophobic speech unchallenged. The racial and racist ideas promoted by these current intellectuals may or may not become accepted in the wider public. This will depend partly on whether these arguments are seen as good explanations and good interpretations for the world around us but more importantly, whether there are other good alternative explanations and interpretations. An example. More homeless people around? Is it because people are getting lazy and waiting to be taken care of by the state or is it because wages received are too low compared to rents paid? Is it because immigrants are taking the jobs from the native population or is it because the Earth's resources are limited with too many of us already?

Is it because we live in a certain social and economic system that cannot provide us all with a good life or is homelessness simply a natural fact of life with no solution? All these are different explanations and interpretations for a single perceived social problem. The acceptance of any of these explanations will depend on people's worldview, on their opinions of others and on various understandings of society, humanity and nature.

In present-day Western society, a very pessimistic view of the world has taken hold of the common imagination and it is based partly on a strong belief that there are no alternatives to what is on offer today. There is a deep mistrust in others; others who are seen as having no free will but as only being determined by external factors such as race, gender, biology, culture, education, society, ideology or an allegedly fixed human nature. Racial thinking is part of this mindset and to challenge it today is to oppose the belief that humans are simply objects completely determined by external circumstances. To promote Enlightenment belief in humanity's potential ability to control its own destiny necessarily leads to the recognition that racial thinking and racist ideas are wrong and need to be completely opposed. Unfortunately, the very radical and revolutionary consequences of Enlightenment ideas are very frightening to those in power and to those benefiting from or accepting our current social order. Ideas, such as anti-racism based on politicized identities, which celebrate our racial differences and thus do not challenge prevalent racial thinking, the status quo and prevailing social organization, will more likely be promoted by those in power.

The Contradictions of the Enlightenment?

One of the most important points for our current discussion about race is that the idea of race, developed in nineteenth-century Western society, is a mechanism for explaining away the mismatch between the Enlightenment notion of equality and the social reality of inequality. If social inequality were to be the result of a natural and racial hierarchy among men, then humanity's potential to challenge this inequality could be rejected as a simple illusion. Social inequalities, which still existed in the new capitalist society, were portrayed as part of a supposed natural and permanent order out of the control of human actions. Enlightenment philosophers had challenged the notion of natural and God-given hierarchies present in the old medieval feudal system but social problems, the fear the ruling elites felt toward the new social force represented by the working class, and the reaction by some intellectuals against the social disorder created by the eighteenth and nineteenth centuries' revolutions, provided the conditions under which racial thinking could be fully developed and accepted.

It is not that some intellectuals sat down and decided to invent the concept of race to justify their actions and/or inaction, but that the social inequalities still present in society were increasingly seen and accepted as natural and permanent, despite the Enlightenment's belief in equality and promise that men, endowed with reason, could take charge of their own destiny and erase all social divisions. The specific social conditions and problems created after the American and French revolutions, the building of nations in Europe and the constant social troubles established a sense of disorder and instability. In this atmosphere, the increasing rejection of the optimism and philosophy of natural universal rights previously advocated by the eighteenth-century Enlightenment allowed the development and acceptance of certain ideas and made race become a reality. In fact, the intellectual reactions to the Enlightenment are the true origins of the ideas which developed to form the concept of race. Race is a social category, produced through this history, through human struggles during these social, intellectual and economic conflicts. Race is not simply an idea or ideology but has real consequences now. To oppose race and racial divisions, we need more than simply to change our mind or our individual attitude.

Enlightenment universalism did not create the racial discourse but developed the idea of natural rights where all humans are equal as opposed to the old belief of a natural hierarchy between humans. As Kenan Malik has noted, Enlightenment philosophers initially understood progress as inevitable, as a result of people challenging traditions, irrational prejudices and superstitions and improving or destroying old institutions. The initial opposition to these ideas and to social change came from a very diverse group of people known as the Romantics. Some of the Romantics did start as supporters of the "common man" seen as suffering terribly from the consequences of capitalist development. The social upheaval that followed the revolutions led them to search for order and stability. They argued that the natural rights would destroy social equilibrium and thus demanded the return of traditions and hierarchy to help restore order.[40]

The idea of race grew, in the second half of the nineteenth century, during a period of important concerns about democracy, vote extensions to the working class, political equality, the meaning of "nation" and "national character," and the building of nations. The internal class divisions within European societies were first rationalized and naturalized through the discourse of race before race became associated with skin color. The concept of race gave expression to the interests of the ruling elite. It gave them a positive sense of superiority over the common people, like in France for example. Georges Vacher de Lapouge appropriated Henri de Boulainvilliers's idea of Frankish and Gallic ancestry to support his sense of superiority. The notion of Frankish and Gallic ancestry, developed in the early eighteenth century, argued that the higher social position of French nobles was down to the fact that they were descendants of the tribe of the Franks, a courageous, self-governing Germanic people. The common people were seen as descendants of the Gallo-Romans who had been conquered by the Franks. Lapouge argued that the cause of the problems in France after its defeat in the Franco-Prussian war, in 1871, was the "dilution of the higher-class dolichocephalic Frankish elements during the French Revolution and their subsequent replacement by the increasing brachycephalic lower-class elements." Essentially, for Lapouge, France was not a community with a single good race but a "multi-racial" community damaged by the common people or lower classes.[41]

In England, for example, Alfred Marshall, considered one of the most influential economists of his time, expressed both his beliefs in the superiority of the upper classes and in the superiority of the British race:

> There can be no doubt that this extension of the English race has been a benefit to the world. A check to the growth of the population would do great harm if it affected only the more intelligent races and particularly the more intelligent classes of these races. There does indeed appear some danger of this evil. For instance, if the lower classes of Englishmen multiply more rapidly than those which are morally and physically superior, not only will the population of England deteriorate, but also that part of the population of America and Australia which descends from Englishmen will be less intelligent that it otherwise would be. Again, if Englishmen multiply less rapidly than the Chinese, this spiritless race will overrun portions of the earth that otherwise would have been peopled by English vigour.[42]

Marshall understood history as the history of races. For him, the economic and social well-being of England and of the world depended on the breeding rate of the upper classes and of the British population.

The view of history as an account of permanent competitions between races also developed from the nineteenth century when history became an academic discipline rather than just a branch of literature. Professional historians wanted to separate their own work they saw as being part of important scientific effort from the work of amateurs seen as storytellers. This trend is seen as having been greatly influenced by German historian Barthold Georg Niebuhr, who reinterpreted the history of the Greeks and the Romans by looking at the character of the people, their kin and kith relationships, their ethnic characteristics, their climate, languages and geographical regions. Developing his conception of natural history, he reinterpreted the political and social world of the Greco-Roman by describing the "natural people" and their languages which, in his view, help us to understand the past. He thought that the way to understand the Greco-Roman past was by looking at racial/ethnic groups and their interactions with each other and their climate rather than by looking at their political character.[43] His work was and is still used widely. History became a series of natural histories described by anthropologists, philologists (studying languages) and historians. Today, history is often understood using natural sciences, psychological and anthropological concepts, and creates natural stories of different types of people and communities that came before us. Our past is less often understood through the historical study of different political and social communities applying political and economic concepts to understand the differences between eras.

Count Arthur Gobineau is another intellectual who developed racial thinking to establish a hierarchy between people in the Western world and those from elsewhere but also to redevelop the belief in natural hierarchy within Western populations. Gobineau, who is often considered the father of scientific racism with his work *Essai sur l'inegalité des races humaines* (1853-55), translated into English as "The Inequality of the Human Races," in 1915, during the First World War, believed that it was unstable racial mixing in particular that was causing the decline of humanity and the fall of civilizations. A French aristocrat and diplomat, an enemy of the ideals of the French Revolution such as equality and democracy, he wrote his essay after the revolutions of 1848, the large and widespread revolts against the European ruling elites. He used Niebuhr's work to argue "that the racial question overshadows all other problems of history, that it holds the key to them all, and that the inequality of the races from whose fusion a people is formed is enough to explain the whole course of its destiny."[44] He believed he was using science and the laws of natural history to explain the collapse of civilizations. Unfortunately for him, the optimism of the Enlightenment still existing at the time of the French publication of his work, the hatred of feudal aristocracy he favored and the contemporary interest in an updated "Might is Right" idea in step with the Darwinian notion of the "survival of the fittest" were temporary obstacles to his ideas. He had to wait 50 years and for the First World War before his doom and gloom ideas (he believed modern civilization was not in any way superior to previous civilizations) became widely and positively received.[45]

If we remember some of the political arguments put forward today, it becomes interesting to note that Gobineau also accounted for the initially poor reception of his book as a result of people refusing to face scientific truth. He claimed he had no interest in the political and moral implications of his doctrines and put his faith entirely in what he thought of as science. In reality, he did not agree with the idea of a "pure race" but thought that the mixing of the three races which he believed existed determines the future for individuals and civilizations. His assessment that civilizations needed a "state of relative stability" led him to argue that no racial mixing would be just as bad as too much racial miscegenation. In his view, white Europeans with their innate reason are beautiful, intelligent and strong while "clearly the Creator was only making a sketch" in creating the "yellow race." In the black race, "the mental faculties are mediocre or even non-existent."[46] However, his belief in the superiority of the white race did not lead him to believe that humanity could ever move toward perfection. His claim that "humanity is not infinitely perfectible" highlights his strong antipathy toward theories of progress.[47]

Slavery not born of racism[48]

The ideology of race and a strong hatred of black people were not the *origins* of modern chattel slavery. In the seventeenth and eighteenth centuries, chattel slavery was not justified using racial arguments but in terms of the economic utility of employing people better suited to hard labor in a hot climate. Previously, slavery was defended under the "Might is Right" doctrine, where the strongest groups conquer the weakest groups and then do as they please with them. Aristotle, for example, justified slavery as a necessity for the continuation of democracy in the city-states to allow citizens the time to involve themselves in politics. In the sixteenth and seventeenth centuries, the discussions about slavery were mainly focused on the excessive cruelty and violence toward slaves; the practice itself was not questioned and many people whom we would consider "white" today, such as Greeks, Slavs or Tartars, were sold on European slave markets before the new development of modern black slavery. We cannot dismiss the importance and specific historical and social conditions of modern slavery by arguing that slavery had existed throughout history and that different groups of people were affected by it. The scale of modern black slavery is, by itself, enough to suggest differences with the past. But I agree with Eric Williams when he noted that slavery "in the Caribbean has been too narrowly identified with the Negro. A racial twist has thereby been given to what is basically an economic phenomenon. Slavery was not born of racism: rather, racism was the consequence of slavery."[49] In his work *Capitalism and Slavery*, he carefully highlighted the different political and economic interests of slave owners, shipbuilders, merchants, capitalists, aristocrats and the political class in his analysis of the role of slavery during the development of capitalism. Very interestingly, he also showed how slavery finally became a problem for fully developed capitalism. This is a point rarely mentioned by other authors because the importance, for the capitalist system, of the availability of "free" workers able to sell their labor is ignored or portrayed as a natural aspect of human life.

Modern slavery occurred in a world where the majority of the European population were unfree and living extremely hard, cruel and short existences. Very harsh treatment, laws, policies and regulations ruthlessly controlling the lower classes were the norm. Prosperity mainly came from the countryside both in Europe and in the colonies, before the full development of capitalism. A great number of the laboring classes was essential for the economy and, for economic reasons, African slaves were often seen as the best option over limited free labor. In the New World, the introduction of monocultures for trade and profit, the move from small farms to large plantations and the limited supply of Native Americans led to the European poor whites first being looked at for a labor supply. Most were indentured servants. The homeless, vagrants, kidnapped poor, convicts or war prisoners such as the Irish prisoners were shipped to the New World. The increasing industrial development in England meant a rising need for its own labor supply at home, limiting the labor supply for the New World. But also the change in the economic structure in the New World, with increasingly larger plantations for tobacco, sugar and cotton, led to even more demands for African slaves.[50]

One of the best known American events, the Bacon's Rebellion, is one of many examples showing that the relationship between different groups of people can be understood only in its historical context. The black/oppressed versus white/

racist/oppressor relationship, portrayed today as natural and permanent due to some supposedly innate characteristics of both whites and blacks or portrayed as the consequence of the original sin inherited by white people, denies the reality of our past. In 1675, Virginia, Bacon's Rebellion first started as a result of a political dispute within the ruling elites of the colony. It was a dispute over a policy concerning Native Americans, between Governor Sir William Berkeley, on behalf of those privileged by the old English regime, and the newer plantation owners led by Nathaniel Bacon. They all agreed with the idea of pushing Native Americans out of the lands for English settlement but not on the timing and rate for it to be done.[51] The Governor needed to keep a friendly relationship with some of the Native American tribes to protect the English settlers but also to have help from the tribes with capturing runaway bond-laborers. The privilege of trading with Native Americans was restricted to only a few of the elites approved by the Governor, creating resentment among other social elites and colonists. Economic problems with tobacco prices and competition from other colonies led plantation owners to blame Native Americans and to demand more lands.

But the rebellion, which originally started as anti-Native American and over demands for more lands, turned into social troubles with increasing political and military power for Bacon and his supporters. In 1676, ordinary settlers and bond-laborers entered the rebellion for their own interests, thus opposing the plantation owners and demanding freedom from servitude. Bacon had promised liberty to all servants and slaves, augmenting the numbers of his rebel followers. Virginian settlers of all classes including people in indentured servitude and slaves and of all backgrounds such as English or African descent joined the rebellion hoping for freedom.[52] They chased the Governor out and torched the capital, Jamestown. The alliance between European-American indentured servants and

African-American slaves and indentured servants, all fighting for freedom and for the abolition of slavery, greatly disturbed the ruling class both in Virginia and England. Despite the increasing number of policies and regulations, already introduced by 1676, against the laborers of African descent with laws such as making black women but not the English women taxable or making it possible for blacks to end up with life servitude rather than years servitude, the rebellion was not a division between races, black and white, but a division between different classes, the laboring classes and the ruling class, who clearly had different interests in liberating servants and slaves. This is important to remember. It also explains the famous statement on the back cover of the book *The Invention of the White Race* by Theodore W. Allen which stated that "(w)hen the first Africans arrived in Virginia in 1619, there were no 'white' people there; nor, according to the colonial records, would there be for another sixty years."[53]

This statement was meant to show that the white race was invented later by the ruling class in order to divide the laboring class. I do not agree that the white race or any other races were *invented* by the ruling class. "Invention" creates too much an idea of a premeditated conscious act by a somehow united ruling class. It can also give the image of a conspiracy theory which is not useful at all. And as seen with Bacon's Rebellion, it was fear that made the ruling class act and create new laws and regulations, not a sense of power. However, the important point here is that the separation between black slaves and white laboring classes did not start because of racism within the white population. In this chapter, I have been trying to explain how race and racial divisions are not natural or invented but are the product of history, of the relationship between intellectual inquiries, social conflicts, and social and economic development. With the Bacon's Rebellion, we see the conflicts within the European ruling class, between the settlers and the Native Americans and between the ruling class and the laboring classes during very difficult economic problems. In response to the social upheaval, the fear of the ruling class led them to introduce more policies and laws to divide the laborers of European descent from laborers of African descent. A white person marrying a black person would be banished from the community. A white woman giving birth to the child of a black man would be fined, have an increase in years of servitude or become an indentured servant for a few years. Free black men could not hold public office anymore. Between 1680 and 1705, new Virginia laws were introduced to completely separate the population according to skin color.

Early black liberation

The movement for black liberation in the French Caribbean at the end of the eighteenth century is a very important historical event to consider when studying the history of liberation movements. But it is also a good example confirming the view that the notion of race is a product of history. The debates around slavery in the eighteenth century show the tension between Enlightenment support for universal rights and the reality of a society where property rights were seen as very important politically, philosophically and socially. There were numerous attempts to reconcile the "rights of slaves with those of slaveholders."[54] Even though our current social and economic circumstances have changed since, we could still reflect upon the numerous attempts to reconcile the rights of workers with those of the capitalist class. But let's go back to the past for another moment and see what we can learn from it.

In the eighteenth century, the majority of the French population in mainland France was not initially interested in the colonies. With no personal economic interests in slavery, and it being a world away, troubles in the colonies were a long distance from the social upheaval they were dealing with at the time. The majority of the population died in the same local rural area in which they were born and had lived throughout their lives. Most could not read, and news came from people, like seasonal laborers and merchants, who had to travel to work. The French state and the Church would impart only news they deemed important for the population to know about.[55] The issue of black slavery was most certainly not of any importance to most of them, except for those living in port cities. The original discussions about slavery, freedom and rights came from the urban upper class. A few Republican democrats, including Brissot and Condorcet, who formed the "Societé des Amis des Noirs" (Society of the Friends of Black People) in Paris on February 19, 1788, demanded the abolition of the slave trade between Africa and the New World and better treatment for slaves.[56] They did not believe that slavery should be ended immediately but gradually, first by stopping the slave trade and forcing owners to keep the remaining slaves healthy. Eventually, once the slaves were deemed ready for freedom and ready to become part of society, they had hoped slavery would become illegal without bloodshed or civil war. Their arguments emerged from the contradiction between supporting equality for black people and the importance of preserving the French economy and property rights. The colonies were essential for the economy of France at the time of developing capitalism because of the weakness of the developing bourgeoisie compared to the continued presence of the still powerful Ancient Regime. The wealth of the new capitalist class was dependent on colonial trade and private property. Abolition of the slave trade and slavery was often opposed using the argument that this abolition would damage France. It was also easy to claim that black equality was being promoted by foreigners intent on attacking France's economy and power in the Caribbean. Britain, for example, which also had interests in the Caribbean world, was a major economic rival of France worldwide.[57] Slave owners argued that black slavery was natural and necessary because whites could not work in the plantations as efficiently as the blacks could. Charles-Louis de Secondat, Baron de le Brede et de Montesquieu, mostly known as Montesquieu, is one of the most famous of the political philosophers of the Enlightenment. While Montesquieu was not a defender of slavery, slave owners used his name and adopted his proposition for their own purpose. He had argued that black slavery might be a necessary evil because certain groups of people might be better adapted to a particular climate than others, leading him to declare that "black slavery seems less shocking to our reason."[58]

While Republican democrats were not pushing for the immediate abolition of slavery, they were arguing for the rights of "free blacks"/"gens de couleur" in the colonies, people with mixed black and white ancestry, who owned property or even slaves. Interestingly, the voting rights of "free blacks" with substantial property were initially approved by the French National Assembly in May 1791 at a time when many poor whites did not have the vote. Support for the radical idea of black emancipation was also quite low among the "free blacks" at first. The "free blacks" who were wealthier than other black people supported the white plantation owners in their opposition to the demand for equality. They did not oppose slavery particularly, given that they often owned slaves themselves. Kenan Malik has explained well the ambivalence about slavery:

It is not racial categorisation but the social needs of modern society that impel it to restrict the concept of equal rights. Economic utility and the desire not to challenge property rights, not racial ideology, gave rise to Western ambivalence about slavery. The particular forms that capitalist society adopted ensured that Enlightenment universalism became degraded in practice. It was through this process that the discourse of race developed.[59]

The history of the Haitian Revolution showed both this ambivalence and the resolution of it when the balance of social power changed. The first uprising on the island of Saint-Domingue (modern-day Haiti) was in October 1790 when a few hundred "free blacks" led by Vincent Ogé, an educated "free black" also described as a quadroon (one-quarter black, three-quarters white French). He was part of a group of "free blacks" who had been lobbying for the French National Assembly to give them the same rights as white plantation owners. Returning angry from France to Saint-Domingue, he organized an insurrection. Captured, he was tortured and publicly executed on the wheel as a deterrent to others but, in fact, the execution increased dissatisfaction among the "free blacks."[60] The Haitian Revolution was nicely described by CLR James in *The Black Jacobins* where he showed how the slaves of Haiti were not just victims of slavery and oppression but became active in fighting for their own liberation. This revolution was one of many other slave rebellions given that slaves have always resisted their enslavement one way or the other, but it was also the most successful of them where the slaves defeated three great powers: France, Britain and Spain. The revolution started with the next insurgency in August 1791 and by 1803 they had finally ended slavery and French control over the colony. Saint Domingue was renamed "Haiti" and declared an independent nation in 1804. The notion of the Rights of Man was put into practice through the transformation of Haitian society.

The story of one of the leaders of the Haitian Revolution, former slave Toussaint Louverture, is worth highlighting here because it emphasizes the universality of human reason and the existence of a human civilization and not just "Western" civilization or "white" civilization. Toussaint Louverture and others, in the end, understood the importance of the ideas promoted by the Enlightenment and the French Revolution for their own particular struggles. They realized the true significance of these ideas and the real consequences they can have when taken to their logical conclusion. The Enlightenment and French Revolution notions of equal rights and universal rights of man became inspirations for their own fight for freedom from slavery. They illustrated the idea that any human being, from any race, culture or identity, can understand and appropriate thoughts coming from other parts of the world. Today, cultures are presented as barriers to understanding each other's ideas when, in fact, we are all capable of hearing an idea, understanding it, making it our own, applying it and letting others know about it.

Jean-Baptiste Belley was used to link the French Revolution with black liberation. A freed slave fighting for black rights, he became the first black deputy in the French National Assembly in September 1793. Anne-Louis Girodet, an artist who wanted to use art for political purposes, painted a portrait of Belley standing next to a bust of Guillaume-Thomas Raynal, Abbé de Raynal (1713-1796) whose famous work "History of the East and West Indies," published in 1770, denounced European cruelty toward the colonial peoples. The portrait became one of the most famous pictures linking the French Revolution and black liberation.[61] The point, again, is that we cannot look at history as a black versus white race competition unless we are willing to read history backward and apply our present-day concerns to people in the past.

Conclusion

Race is a product of history and it is a relatively new concept. It fully developed only in the nineteenth century. It goes against the concept of politics and a man-made world. The reason I spent so much time trying to show these points is because they challenge many of the current but wrong notions of race used in the anti-racism debates. The history of the idea of race contradicts opinions describing race as an innate characteristic of human nature or of white people, as an original sin, as a disease or as an invention by the ruling class or by white people. But it is also essential to capture these points if we do want to understand why racial thinking seems so vital to Western society today and if we want to finally transcend these horrible racial divisions.

During the nineteenth and twentieth centuries, the idea of race became widely supported by intellectuals and thinkers. Race did not simply serve to distinguish white Europeans from non-white people from other parts of the world. It was not always simply defined by skin color. Some believed that groups such as the lower classes within the white European "race" were from distinct races. The racialization of various groups of people or treating groups of people as if they were races has not stopped. In contemporary society, different categories of people like the Muslims, the Jews and various groups of immigrants like the Eastern Europeans have been treated as if they were separate races. In the next chapter, we will see why it is still possible to do this today.

The new biological definitions of mankind, the need to justify the colonization of the non-Western world, the Atlantic Slave Trade, the conditions of the new working class and the continuous social inequality led to the eventual acceptance of the notion of race that linked biological factors seen as important, such as skin color or cranial capacity and size, to cultural customs.

Many Enlightenment philosophers thought progress was inevitable if human reason and actions were promoted. The loss of Enlightenment optimism led, unfortunately, to an understanding of the world, society and progress as simply results of laws of nature. The Declaration of the Rights of Man, even though they are natural rights, gave expression to the willingness to challenge old notions of social, natural and religious hierarchy. It provided the arguments for the liberation of the politically and socially unequal lower classes. But the limits and reality of the new capitalist society with social inequalities still very much existing led to the acceptance that these inequalities are permanent and natural and led to the development of race. Kenan Malik made a very crucial point when he argued that "inequality is not the product of racial differences" but that in fact, "the perception of racial difference arises out of the persistence of social inequality."[62] To understand the recent development of race and the modern reality of race, we need to understand the limitations of the capitalist society and its own deep divisions and inequalities within humanity.

In the next chapter, I will to try to show how part of our basic understanding of the world, of humans, of society and of nature underlying the race concept, has unfortunately not changed when "race" was replaced by "culture" and "identity." I am not saying that the world has not progressed and that it is the same old, same old but that some of the underlying views of the relationship between humans, society and nature have stayed the same. I am arguing that an anti-political position and thus a fundamental anti-human sentiment underlies all these concepts.

Chapter 2

Determinism and Fatalism in Race and Culture

Alexis de Tocqueville and Gobineau, after meeting in France, became friends and had many years of sustained correspondence even though their ideas were quite irreconcilable. Alexis Charles Henri Clérel, Viscount de Tocqueville, was a French political thinker and historian who is best known for his work *Democracy in America*, one of the most influential books of the nineteenth century. He attacked Gobineau's beliefs that behavior and moral qualities are causally determined by race. He argued that Gobineau's "fatalistic" position leads to "a vast limitation, if not a complete abolition, of human liberty."[1] Alexis de Tocqueville was right with his objections to Gobineau's doctrines. The strong deterministic and fatalistic assumptions underlying the concept of race are anti-human. The belief that belonging to a specific race causally determines behavior and outlook, moral and mental qualities, leaves very little or no room for human reason. A racial outlook ends up denying the potential for free will and agency and the possibility for human beings to determine their own future. It leaves no room for autonomy, morality or for a moral conscience. It allows no possibilities for conscious social change and for reaching freedom. The racial outlook denies the Enlightenment belief in human perfectibility and in universalism. This thinking is based on an anti-human sentiment. Humans are seen mainly as objects, inanimate and passive, acted upon by external factors with no acknowledgment of their quality as subjects, with a mind and an ability to act independently, to consciously decide and to transform their present and future. The argument I am making in this chapter is that this is the case also with the current promotion and celebration of cultural differences. I am not saying that the concepts of race and of culture are the same. "Races" are seen as permanent groups with biological differences leading to a notion of hierarchy. "Cultures" are seen as permanent groups with historical and man-made differences (such as traditions) where the notion of hierarchy is mostly rejected today.

Our ability to reason, our moral conscience and our autonomy are all denied by several political sides today including the side promoting racial and racist ideas, the self-proclaimed gatekeepers of cultures who claim to defend our cultural heritage and the side purporting to fight against racism by demanding diversity, representation and respect of cultural and identity differences. The constant relationship between humans as subjects and humans as objects is forgotten by those promoting a fatalistic quality for race, culture, identity or other external deterministic factors. "The materialist doctrine," Karl Marx noted, "that men are products of circumstances and upbringing, and that, therefore, changed men are products of other circumstances and changed upbringing, forgets that it is men that change circumstances and that the educator himself needs educating."[2] Marx did not fully support the abstract humanism and universalism of the Enlightenment philosophers discussed in this book because he recognized that a chimney sweeper and a factory owner are not equals in our current society. But more importantly, he realized the limitations of these abstract notions which do not recognize or challenge the social barriers preventing the potential full development of humanity and of individuals' abilities.

Humans are created both from external, out-of-their-control factors influencing them and shaping them and from their own capacity to act on external factors as well as on themselves. We, humans, are not simply individual mouthpieces for particular races, cultures or identities but are persons capable of making our own decisions, acting upon them and being responsible for our actions. Our individual moral conscience and our reason are denied when race, culture, identity or social circumstances are seen as factors generating our fates.

In his book *Race: The History of an Idea in the West*, Ivan Hannaford had a very interesting and, in my opinion very important, argument. He argued that there are, at least, two distinct approaches to social organization. Humans can use political thought or racial thought in order to organize themselves as well as to interpret the world around them. Through discussing and analyzing many historical figures involved in political and racial thought, Hannaford argued that racial thinking developed and became increasingly important when political thought and attitude, first created by the ancient Greeks, was gradually abandoned by Western society.[3] The numerous politicized identities such as the racial, cultural and national identities currently intervening in our political debates indicate that Hannaford was right on this point and that we are still in a very anti-political period. Politics cannot exist without the notion of human agents using their capacity for reason in order to understand the world and to organize collectively their own man-made world. The point made by Tocqueville concerning the limitation to human liberty and Hannaford's point on racial thinking and political thought are linked to the same concept of human as subjects of history. Human beings are not simply objects acted upon by external forces. Humans need to be viewed as persons with the capacity for reason, who are able to transform their social, economic and cultural world and who have an active role in fighting for more freedom in order to create a better world for themselves.

I agree with Hannaford's point about race being anti-political but I disagree with him and others who put the blame for racial thinking and racism at the feet of the Enlightenment.[4] The reasonable disagreement over who first initiated racial thinking is often overshadowed by the wrong belief that individuals who first developed racial thinking are then responsible for what happened later. This belief demonstrates a fatalistic attitude. We analyze all previous intellectual and philosophical influences in order to comprehend how and why racial thinking and racism exist now but the present is not the inevitable consequence of what happened yesterday. This should not be considered a cause and effect discussion but a discussion about origins of ideas and of influences. Ideas on their own do not make history but they are, of course, important. Social and economic forces also intervene in history, but ideas can make people act. They can make people accept or reject events, actions and other people. This is one of the reasons we need to argue for the importance of understanding other people's ideas. Another reason is that we know our own ideas well enough only when we understand others' ideas. John Stuart Mill rightly maintained:

> However unwillingly a person who has a strong opinion may admit the possibility that his opinion may be false, he ought to be moved by the consideration that however true it may be, if it is not fully, frequently, and fearlessly discussed, it will be held as a dead dogma, not a living truth.[5]

Ideas that are not challenged and discussed often lose important meanings and become dogma and empty words. By ignoring others' contradictory ideas, we lose the ability to rationally argue for our own ideas.

Thus, the fact that some intellectuals, considered as part of the Enlightenment, had discussed human diversities and had proposed a certain hierarchy between groups does not mean that they developed the concept of race or that they are responsible for contemporary racial thinking. The discussions about human variation in the eighteenth century were still influenced by the Enlightenment's beliefs in the perfectibility of humanity, in progress, in universalism and in social equality. These beliefs had to be abandoned to give the space for the concept of race to fully develop. Besides, the notion of equality first had to be developed and supported in society before rational explanations for the remaining inequalities became necessary. The world was vastly unequal before, with relationships such as master-servant or landlord-serf. Inequality was seen as a fact of life, given by nature or God. Enlightenment thinking helped in developing a society where social inequality was seen as a phenomenon that could be changed by the actions of human beings. The fact that social inequalities persisted after the social transformation into the new capitalist societies led to an increasing belief that maybe these inequalities were natural and permanent after all. This sense of inevitability allowed the full development of racial thinking. Understanding humanity as divided into natural and fixed groups, where members have predetermined moral and mental capabilities, with no room for them to use their reason to improve themselves and where some groups have no abilities for progress, differs from Enlightenment thinking. Please note that I do not agree with the notion of seeing liberalism as the heir to Enlightenment and thus I am only referring to the Enlightenment ideals here.

In *An Answer to the Question: "What is Enlightenment?"*, Immanuel Kant, one of the most influential philosophers of the Western world, responded:

Enlightenment is man's emergence from his self-incurred immaturity. Immaturity is the inability to use one's own understanding without the guidance of another. The immaturity is self-incurred if its cause is not lack of understanding, but lack of resolution and courage to use it without the guidance of another. The motto of enlightenment is therefore: *Sapere aude!* (Dare to be wise) Have courage to use your own understanding![6]

Kant was upholding the importance of reason in order for us to question and understand the world around us. Baron d'Holbach, one of the most radical Enlightenment philosophers, argued that we needed to "attack at their source the prejudices of which the human race has been so long the victim."[7]

Besides, Jonathan Israel argues that the Enlightenment was in fact a battleground between two wings, the "moderate" and "radical" Enlightenment who oppose each other on important questions. Considering the American Revolution, he argues that the two streams were fighting over "democratic versus aristocratic republicanism, support of, versus rejection of, universal rights, citizenship for all versus limited suffrage" as well as discussing "the place of religious authority in society." These intellectual disagreements also led in practice to questions such as whether to reform the "existing social, legal, and institutional order" or to replace it. The moderate wing was the one which managed to become mainstream, according to Israel. Voltaire or Lord Kames, as seen in the previous chapter on racial theories, were part of the mainstream Enlightenment. Philosopher Denis Diderot, philosopher and mathematician Marquis de Condorcet, philosopher Baruch Spinoza and political philosopher Thomas Paine, for example, were seen as radical Enlightenment thinkers.[8] I am not sure if the Enlightenment can be divided so neatly into two sides but it does suggest the variety of philosophical and political views within what is called the Enlightenment.

My focus on the Enlightenment is partly due to the fact that the concept of race fully developed historically after this period. But more importantly, I hope to highlight some of the positive ideas and ideals that have been abandoned to leave the space for the concepts of race, culture and identity to be developed and accepted today. The Enlightenment can be understood as part of a European period where "humanism," which puts humanity at the center of history and society, was actively developing. There were individual European humanists, such as Francesco Petrarca, the Florentine scholar and poet in the fourteenth century. These early humanists were interested in the past and in the intellectual discovery of the Greek and Latin writing. The Enlightenment period expressed a certain humanism in the belief that humanity can understand the world and have access to the truth with human reason rather than simply obeying traditions, religious beliefs and prejudices. Humanism was expressed later in other ways, for example with Karl Marx the revolutionary humanist and one of the most important intellectuals of the last two centuries, who claimed that "Men make their own history, but do not make it just as they please; they do not make it under circumstances chosen by themselves, but under circumstances directly encountered, given and transmitted from the past."[9] With his analysis of the capitalist mode of production, Marx tried to redefine the notion of universalism from the Enlightenment ideals which are often described as too abstract and forgetful of concrete reality, with a conception of the particular and historically specific social reality.

So, looking at Enlightenment ideals, we can see how humanist sentiments have been degraded or abandoned in our current society. This is crucial because the way we define different groups of human beings and how we understand the relationships between these varied groups has a direct connection with how we conceive humanity and comprehend the relationship between humans, society and nature. The way we see ourselves and others strongly influences the ideas we will develop in order to resolve social issues. If you believe people cannot be trusted, you are more likely to support ideas that will control others rather than policies that give them the space to make their own decisions. It is also linked to the visions and hopes we have for the future. We cannot fight racial thinking without a humanist vision and this vision, expressed well in Martin Luther King, Jr's speech "I have a dream..."[10], is conspicuous by its absence in mainstream identity-based anti-racism movement. I am not advocating that we deny the existence of racial and social divisions today and their consequences. Claiming that race is not important is clearly denying reality. Belonging to a specific racial group has consequences and impacts our lives and experiences. But we need to recognize our ability to reason and think of ways to organize ourselves differently in order to transcend our current racial divisions. We know that social transformations have occurred in our past, for example with a feudal society changed into a capitalist society. The question is how we can go further in order to resolve our racial and other social divisions.

I need to add that I do not mean humanism as anti-religious which is the way it is often understood today but as recognizing humanity's achievement in the past and as realizing humanity's potential in deciding and acting for its future. The "importance of fighting a humanist vision" are not just empty words when we look at the very common portrayal of humans as parasites, as greedy and selfish beings, as a disease contaminating Earth, as the destructive force in nature that needs to be eliminated or contained. Some of the responses in the story of Harambe the gorilla and the 3-year-old child are good examples.[11] The killing of the gorilla to save the 3-year-old boy, who had managed to climb into the zoo enclosure, led to many people questioning the necessity to kill an individual from an endangered species in order to save a child from a species with 7 billion other members. We live at a time when the value of human life is seen as negligible. The reaction or more exactly the lack of general reaction about the deaths of immigrants at the doors of Fortress Europe is another example of the contemporary low regard given to human life. Should other human beings be treated as if they are worth less than animals because they have not got the right nationalities or are not citizens of a powerful nation? In what way can one claim to fight against injustice, oppression or racism when one does not value human life?

Origin of the modern concept of culture

Kenan Malik remarked that the philosophical idea of the "inner voice" started with Enlightenment philosophers such as Immanuel Kant, but that the focus on the individual "inner voice" was further developed through the counter-Enlightenment stream called Romanticism. This notion helped in elaborating the concept of plurality of cultures and the belief that history can only be grasped through understanding the specificity of "true people" forming particular cultures. Kant believed that the source of our morality could be found within our inner self, in our own minds, not from God or from nature. The Romantics' emphasis on the individual but their refusal to accept the Enlightenment's focus on reason, preferring an emphasis on emotion and imagination, developed the idea of a fixed inner essence.[12] This Romantic inner essence is believed to be attributed before birth and not developed. The inner essence is also not universal but particular to groups of people or unique to individuals. This explanation is very simplistic, but it gives a sense of how ideas can be appropriated and recast. Kant did believe that the source of morality was the moral individual, the moral agent. This is not the case when one believes that race or culture is the principal force determining an individual. From these important philosophical enquiries about the nature of knowledge and the basis of morality, theorists for racial thinking later developed a notion of an inner essence shared by a specific community, causally determined by race and culture. True nobility or the true people of a specific nation would have a distinct inner essence from people of other cultures, races or nations. According to some, a Jewish French citizen did not have the same inner essence as a non-Jewish French citizen did.

France, in the seventeenth century, under King Louis XIV also known as the Sun King, was the leading European power. Its culture was promoted as the highest standard one should imitate and achieve. But in the eighteenth century, other

European societies such as Britain wanted to resist French cultural hegemony and despotism. Britain had already achieved more political liberties than all the other monarchies and feudal systems. Thus, it turned to the idea of rediscovering ancient traditions, literature and other arts. To challenge the hegemony of French classicism in the arts, the British and other nations started to build new national cultures, based on rediscovered and invented old ones, understood as folk cultures today. These discoveries were also often related to communities from the North of Europe. New national histories were formed from the "barbaric" Celtic, Germanic, Scandinavian cultures of the past with their popular songs, poems, superstitions, traditions.[13]

Yet German Romanticism had also a big influence on the current meaning of "culture." Johann Gottfried von Herder, eighteenth-century German philosopher, was one of the most influential thinkers because he was also one of the most coherent in developing these ideas. Herder rejected Enlightenment universalism. He argued that there was a common biological humanity but that human groups separated and diversified into distinct people during social evolution. The real spirit and true culture of a nation come from the spirit and culture of a particular people who are part of the lower classes and live in the countryside, not from notions developed by intellectuals. He saw language as a common human characteristic and argued that each different language was the lived expression of the people's spirit and the sum of all their ancestors.[14] Each culture or society is formed by a people with a unique and specific character defined by their language, history, way of life, myths and legends. A specific individual has a spiritual relationship with a specific people, a "*Volk*" bound by language, traditions, ritual and history.[15] In his view, a foreigner cannot really learn another language because it is linked to the soul of a particular people. History for him became a history of different cultures or more exactly, a history of variations between the cultures. He thought that there were no absolute, no universal and timeless standards and norms in order for us to judge human creations. All had to be judged within a particular context and "each historical period and nation corresponded to a specific type of humanity" with "its independent existence" and "individual reason."[16] He did not accept racial thinking, nor did he believe in hierarchy of cultures or nations. He was against despotism and intolerance. Because of his beliefs in a spirit of the people, he thought that new states, created through war and the combining of different people, were not right. Still, we will see later that his arguments were used in the development of racial theory advanced by others and as inspirations to actions such as the Third Reich or Nazi Germany.[17]

The support for Herder's ideas started in Germany after the total defeat of the old Prussian army by Napoleon in 1806. This defeat and resulting French domination led to the search for an approach able to unite the German nation against the occupation. French universalism, promoted as a force which would bond and benefit all countries conquered by Napoleon, became a focus for resentment not only in Germany. This universalism mixed with French ethnocentrism argued that French society was the best representative of humanity. But despite this claim, France had not been able to eradicate social divisions in France, let alone in Germany and elsewhere. Thus, sections of the German elites started to see French universalism not as liberating but as a foreign attempt to dominate Germany. By developing Herder's ideas, German nationalists tried to create a sense of German unity and uniqueness through the idea of "the Spirit of the German people."

As we can see the original modern notion of culture was first developed with the concept of the nation. In order to understand the relationship between race and culture, we need to look at the concept of nation. As mentioned before, the concept of race was applied to explain divisions within European and

American nations. The divisions between the lower classes and upper classes were explained as natural and permanent racial divisions. A description of the British Bethnal Green poor as "a caste apart, a race of whom we know nothing, whose lives are of quite different complexion from ours, persons with whom we have no point of contact"[18] was no more unusual than the claims by Scottish anatomist Robert Knox that "the Celtic race does not, and never could be made to comprehend the meaning of the word liberty." Knox went further in voicing his opinions about the Irish Catholics by declaring the "source of all evil lies *in the race*, the Celtic race of Ireland. There is no getting over historical fact." He then concluded that the "race must be forced from the soil; by fair means, if possible; still they must leave. England's safety requires it."[19] It is interesting to note the justification that "England's safety requires it" given that this is still the kind of justification used by some people against newcomers. This view of the Irish as a separate race was also exported from Britain to the United States even though the separation between white and black race was already well established there.

The fully developed concept of race was also applied to discuss the differences between nations, especially the divisions between European societies and the rest of the world, including their colonies. The domination of Western nations over the other societies and nations was explained by the presumed superiority of the white race over the other races. Race became central to Western elites' sense of superiority and identity. Many today see the world divided into nations as something that has always been so. But the modern concept of nation and the building of nations are relatively recent phenomena. I think it is useful to look at the historical origin and definitions of the concept of nation as well as the social, economic and historical forces intervening during the period of nation-building if we want to understand the contemporary relationship between race, nation and culture.

Origin of the modern concept of the nation

The modern concept of the nation as a *political* entity emerged in France, in the mid-eighteenth century, to challenge the feudal hierarchy and the power of the aristocracy. The concept evolved during the attempt by the French bourgeoisie to overthrow the Ancient Regime and replace it with a Republic and a capitalist system. This political concept, in the original meaning, was based on the idea that all people living on the territory voluntarily form the nation together. It was centered around the ideas of Enlightenment and on the *Social Contract* of Jean-Jacques Rousseau, one of the most influential philosophers of Western society but also an ambiguous opponent of the Enlightenment. The concept promotes the notion of a citizenship where all citizens regardless of class, birth privilege or ethnicity would be sovereign, would have rights and be allowed to participate in the life of the state.[20] The nation was thus conceived as a voluntary and political community of citizens, based on our ability for reason and free will. The sovereignty and authority of the king, given by God, was to be supplanted by the sovereignty and authority of the people as a whole. There is no doubt that this is a very radical conception of nation which seems quite foreign to us today. The strangeness shows how far we have moved from the original concept. I think it is based on wishful thinking or an illusion to argue that nations today represent the sovereign people. It is also ignoring what happened between the time the original concept was formulated and our reality today. All democratic nation-states today have strong restrictions on the power of the people and are certainly not voluntary political associations based on reason and commitment. It is interesting to note that even common language was not used initially to define a nation. The notion of a national language itself developed from nationalism. In France, as late as 1860, it is thought that about half of the French population was still learning French as a foreign language.[21] In fact, English-born American political theorist

Thomas Paine was elected to the French National Convention, in the new French Republic in 1792, even though he did not speak French. I think it is very useful to have a common language with which we can all communicate easily. But the current demand for a common language, seen as a tool for social cohesion, is simply a diversion or technical solution to a political and social problem. We may think it normal today to define a nation by a common language or common ethnicity but that is not how the political concept and purpose of the nation were originally developed and understood.

American nationhood was also originally developed with the notion of the sovereign people or popular sovereignty against colonial domination, for the common good against privilege, for equality and universalism. Eric Hobsbawm noted that:

> we cannot therefore read into the revolutionary "nation" anything like the later nationalist programme of establishing nation-states for bodies defined in terms of the criteria so hotly debated by the nineteenth-century theorists, such as ethnicity, common language, religion, territory and common historical memories.[22]

The concept of self-determination and the demand for the right to form their own nation have been useful in the fight for liberation and access to rights by some groups of people, previously living under the domination of others. But if we look at all the different communities in the world who did not get their own nations, it is clear that these concepts can be used to cohere a movement but can also be used to deny the freedom of others. The world distribution of political power at a particular time and the specific social and economic contexts will contribute to the liberation of some groups and not others. The Haitian Revolution was not based on nationalism, national culture and national identity and yet the slaves succeeded. They fought for freedom, demanding that the notion of natural rights be applied to them too. But then, the critique of the modern notion of nation and nationalism is not based only on the known consequences such as the use by some liberation movements or the promotion of Nazism. It is about recognizing the link between nation, culture, race and the anti-political and anti-human world these ideas create. Many good and bad ideas can have good and bad social consequences at a particular time.

Now, if we are interested in challenging racism by transcending racial and cultural divisions and building a universalist political position, we cannot avoid the issues around the concept of the nation. The original concept of the nation was partly developed by the Enlightenment but the universal Man of Enlightenment, the rational individual with free will, is contradicted by the particularistic notion of citizen/non-citizen, defined by geography and nationality. What is worse is that, today, nationality and citizenship had become mainly defined by culture, race, birthplace, ancestry or legal concepts. Maxim Silverman was right when he remarked:

> This contradiction appears even more marked when one remembers that it was precisely the break with privilege and particular interests and the creation of a common good that were central to the Revolutionary ideal. By defining the common good within the exclusive framework of the nation, the Revolution crystallised the tension between universalism and particularism of the Enlightenment.[23]

The universalism of the Enlightenment was an abstract notion which could not resolve the contradiction at the time. We now live in a different social and economic world with more people able to access humanity's increasing knowledge and with better possibilities in learning from other attempts at defining a universalist position.

Other notions of the "nation"

As we saw, German nationhood, for example, was not a "revolutionary nation" and developed later in the nineteenth century. It was based on particularism as opposed to universalism, on a special people bound by blood and heredity and a specific German soul. It developed in opposition to Napoleon and the promoted French universalism as seen above. The differences between France and Germany's original understanding of the nation has led some people to define the original French meaning of nation as "civic nation," based on the universalist ideas of the French Enlightenment while describing the original German meaning as "ethnic nation," based on the particularism of German Romanticism. This is in order to make a distinction between a voluntary community of citizens versus a community of people together because they are defined by common races or ethnicities. This distinction between France and Germany is a myth. French nationalism, with the French Revolution, started by being based on an ethnocentric universalism with the idea that France would show the world the best ways to think and live. The political definition of citizenship was lost very quickly, at the beginning of the French Revolution. In the nineteenth century, behind other nations such as Britain and Germany which had already advanced in this direction, its nationalism changed and developed on an invented definition of French history and culture.

By the mid-nineteenth century, Enlightenment ideals and French universalism supported by the revolutionaries were rejected by most. The French opponents had been arguing that this notion of a common humanity had created too much social upheaval and a complete destruction of social order. Joseph de Maistre, one of the most formidable French opponents of the French Revolution, and who was against the view that mankind was universal, had already famously declared in 1797: "There is no such thing as *man* in the world. During my life I have seen

Frenchmen, Italians, Russians. Thanks to Montesquieu, I even know that *one can be Persian*. But as for *man*, I declare that I have never in my life met him; if he exists, he is unknown to me." He was arguing that people were born into particular societies and that from birth, they had to socialize and organize life and behavior according to the customs, rules and traditions of this particular society. People do not choose to be part of a community but are born into it. Destroying traditions and old institutions in order to create a nation based on equality, free association and universal rights would be, according to him, akin to destroying the nation's soul and identity.[24] The particular culture found in a community, society or nation should be preserved because it embodies the group's identity. Anti-Enlightenment thinking is at the root of the concept of culture and nation we are familiar with today.

The defeat of France in the Franco-Prussian War of 1870-1871, the fall of the Second Empire replaced by the third Republic, the bloody suppression of the Paris Commune, the increased fear of the working class/"masses" experienced by the elites and the demand to give the Alsace and Lorraine regions to the Germans really changed the conversations about the meaning of the nation. Of course, the original French meaning had already been rejected with Napoleon and his empire. In 1882, Ernest Renan, a famous French philologist, gave a celebrated lecture at the Sorbonne in Paris called "What is a Nation?" Renan was rejecting biological race, language, geography, religion as significant factors to understanding a nation. To challenge the Germans, who were demanding the Alsace and Lorraine regions be given back to them on ethnic justifications, he argued that race had "no application in politics" and that "the greatest European nations are nations of essentially mixed blood." He reasoned that a nation is a living soul made of two parts, one in the past and one in the present. The part in the past is made of a rich common heritage, while the part in the present is the current consent to live together and the will to carry on promoting this undivided common heritage. He believed that an individual, like a nation, is the result of common sacrifices, efforts and caring and that the cult of the nation's ancestors is right. "Our ancestors made us what we are," he claimed and, "we are what you were; we will be what you are."[25] Renan was arguing that a nation is formed of individuals with a common history and ancestry and with the willingness to carry on together the traditions of these ancestors. According to him, the consent to live together comes from the common heritage and common ancestry. He was promoting the idea that a common inherited culture, rather than language, race or ethnicity should define a nation. This is a conception of the nation where "race" is replaced by "culture." In Renan's concept, we do not have rational individuals consenting to live together and accepting their role in the life of the state, with rights and duties. This is the opposite of the Enlightenment ideals that had promoted the use of reason above obedience of traditions, customs, prejudices and old hierarchy. If we argue that organizing ourselves through race is anti-political, then we have to also agree that organizing ourselves around obeying traditions from a common ancestry is anti-political. Furthermore, it is worth remembering that communities based on kinship, clans and families are pre-political communities based on pre-political attachments, not political entities based on the agency and commitment of rational individuals to collectively work for the common good.

The idea of the nation during the "revolutionary democratic" period[26] was originally based on the Enlightenment belief in a common humanity with a single culture. Various groups may not have been at the same level in human culture at that particular time but there was a belief that all would, eventually, join it at the same level and that the differences would disappear. The idea of the nation by the end of the nineteenth century was entirely based on the rejection of a common human culture.

Maurice Barrès, a French author and politician and an outspoken nationalist, believed that France was "definitely not a race but a nation" but also added "Alas! There is no French race, but a French people, a French nation," showing his unhappiness that there was no French race to consider.[27] For him, "a nation is the shared possession of an ancient cemetery and the will to continue to maintain the prominence of that undivided heritage."[28] More importantly for our discussion here is that he believed that this specific French heritage, that belonging to a specific nation, completely determined people's thoughts and acts. According to him, we cannot really escape from our nation or culture. He made this clear when claiming: "If I were to be naturalized as a Chinese and conform scrupulously to the prescriptions of Chinese law, I would not stop forming French ideas and associating them in French."[29] The complete rejection of the existence of a common human culture was undoubtedly clear when he argued that, "German truth and English truth have nothing to do with French truth" and that, "they can poison us."[30]

The nineteenth century was the age of nation-building where many European nations became fully formed. During the "Age of Revolution" (1789-1848) and excluding the French Revolution, Eric Hobsbawm defined three main waves of revolutions between 1815 and 1848. The period 1820-1824 saw the social upheaval mainly in the Mediterranean region: Spain, Naples and Greece. Between 1829 and 1834, the events affected all Western Europe (west of Russia) when the Bourbons in France were overthrown, and the Belgium Revolution led to Belgium independence from the Netherlands. The biggest wave was the revolutions of 1848 affecting many European countries such as France, the German states, the whole of Italy, Switzerland, Spain, Ireland and Britain. The nineteenth century was a period of great social and political upheaval and transformation. The 1830s saw the final defeat of the aristocracy by the bourgeoisie in Western Europe and the emergence of nationalist movements in many European countries. The working class also started to become a social and political force in Britain and France.[31] All these events revealed deep divisions and inequalities within Western societies which led to a fear of change within the upper classes and a demand for order. Society, social issues, inequalities, hierarchies and order started to be explained with laws of nature which physical anthropologists and other naturalists described. God was replaced by nature. The notion of order, equilibrium and design in nature was applied to society. Social Darwinism put natural, scientific processes as "the guarantor of social equilibrium" rather than God, who was increasingly rejected.[32]

Racial science in trouble

In the nineteenth and early twentieth centuries, divisions and inequalities were seen as natural. Racial and natural theories claiming the authority of science were used to interpret the world. Race became the main way Western political elites explained their assumed superiority over the world and justified their pretended civilizing mission. Political, social and economic inequalities between nations, international events and conflicts were described and interpreted as the consequences of inequalities between races or as the degeneration of particular races.

The word eugenics, from the Greek words for "well born," was coined by Francis Galton in 1883. He wanted to give "the more suitable races or strains of blood a better chance of prevailing speedily over the less suitable."[33] His aim in improving the physical and mental level of the human race, with the help of state intervention, was based on the notion that certain people did have better physical and mental qualities than others and that these people should be encouraged to breed faster than others.[34] In essence, his aim was centered around his belief in perfection and a fixed human nature. He imagined a close-ended future where humanity would have eventually created the best human possible according to certain criteria (his maybe) rather than the open-ended notion of perfectibility promoted by the Enlightenment. The international eugenics movement was very influential in the early twentieth century until World War 2. It appealed to people across the political spectrum and across nations. Scientists from quite a few fields of study such as genetics, psychology, biology, anthropology and sociology were involved in the eugenics movement throughout the Western world. Not all in the movement were supporting or working on racial theories. Some focused on what they thought were "degenerates" such as mentally-ill people or people with mental and/or physical characteristics seen as outside the acceptable norms. Family studies were, for example, another interest. These studies were used to justify sterilization in order to stop the fast reproduction of "degenerates." The most famous study was done on the Kallikak family by Henry Herbert Goddard who later distanced himself from it. It was to show the differences in mental and physical qualities between the descendants of a single soldier who had an illegitimate child with a "feebleminded tavern wench" and legitimate children with a "respectable girl of good family."[35]

The early twentieth century also saw an increasing lack of confidence in the idea of "white race" superiority and a weakening of the influence of scientific racism and racial theories. But Christopher Kyriakides and Rodolfo D Torres, in their book *Race Defaced: Paradigms of Pessimism, Politics of Possibility*, made an important point, in relation to some of the current race discussions, when they argued that "whiteness" as an identity was intrinsically weak. As seen before, white lower classes had fought in solidarity with black lower classes against the white ruling class. The authors provided several other cases in order to demonstrate their point:

Whiteness is intrinsically weak – fractured in its origin – and it is only after we are able to grasp the internal weakness of whiteness that we begin to understand the relative strength of racial doctrine. The power of limitation it placed on possibility was related not to the strength of whiteness but to the prior defeat of the radically subjective.[36]

The problem is not the power of whiteness. It is the anti-humanist sentiment and ideas which undermined the notion of human beings as autonomous agents able to act on their destiny. Talks about whiteness and blackness or white working class and black working class often do not try to understand why there is a division between the two groups of people. It is already assumed that the divisions have always existed as if there is an intrinsic aspect of ourselves that divides us or as if the ruling class simply invented the divisions and the rest of the population had meekly acquiesced.

But the rise of the working class, the increasing power of their movement with a growth in trade unionism and the demand for more democracy, had led to questions about the racial superiority of the elites over the lower classes. The weakness of the notion of "white unity" was further shown with the Anglo-Japanese Alliance of 1902. This was the first time a European power, Britain, had an alliance with an Asian power, Japan, to counter a Western rival, Russia. The Treaty of Alliance between the German Empire and the Ottoman Empire on August 2, 1914 and the presence of black soldiers during the war also undermined white solidarity.[37] The military victory of Japan over Russia in 1905 was seen by many in the West not simply as the result of a conflict between two nations but as a humiliation of a "white nation" by a "non-white nation" and a threat to the "existing balance of racial power."[38] The growing resistance to Western domination in the colonies and the rise of Third World nationalism, especially after the Second World War, led to further undermining of racial theories. Elazar Barkan in The

Retreat of Scientific Racism thoroughly showed the reluctance of the American and British scientists in abandoning the concept of race between the world wars.[39] They were influenced like everybody else by the social and political contexts in which they lived but eventually had to distance themselves from it. The events that created a particular dislike for racial theories were the Second World War and the Holocaust.

The Nazis seized power in Germany in 1933 and the German racial hygienists were able to introduce their eugenics laws within the first 6 months, with an increasing racial focus against Jews and others after the introduction. The international eugenics movement and in particular the American eugenicists had given them important theoretical, scientific, practical and social information about eugenics laws. But one of the complaints from German eugenicists was the incoherence with which these laws were applied in the United States. A close relationship between American and German eugenicists had developed after the First World War and, by 1930, had taken over the leadership place from Great Britain. That relationship was financial; for example, with the Rockefeller foundation. But it also included the transfer of scientific, medical and political knowledge.[40] By 1933, the American eugenics movement had provided quite a few examples of sterilization and immigration laws that aimed to improve the population. The United States Supreme Court in 1927, for example, had decided that, in order to prevent "being swamped with incompetents," compulsory sterilization was constitutional. They had argued:

It is better for all the world if instead of waiting to execute degenerate offspring for crime, or to let them starve for their imbecility, society can prevent those who are manifestly unfit from continuing their kind. The principle that sustained compulsory vaccination is broad enough to cover the cutting of the Fallopian tubes.[41]

The American Immigration Act of 1924 was approved by many in the German eugenics movement even though eugenics concerns, the mental tests, were not the basis of this 1924 act. Hans F K Guenther, a famous German race anthropologist, celebrated it as an act meant to prevent both degenerate individuals and some ethnic groups from entering the United States.[42] The Nazi effort in improving the "German race" was itself interpreted by the international eugenics movement as the first nationwide attempt to adopt their ideology and implement their "practical proposals." They had been asking their own government to be more "eugenically minded." With the experience of the eugenics movement behind them, the Nazi government introduced several laws and regulations very quickly such as the "Law against Dangerous Habitual Criminals" for the sterilization and castration of criminals, the "Decree for the Granting of Marriage Loans," passed in July 1933 allowing "funding to non-Jewish couples free of mental or physical illness." The "Law on Preventing Hereditarily Ill Progeny," for the sterilization of people with physical and mental "problems," passed in July 1933 in Germany and enacted in January 1934, was influenced by analyses of the Californian sterilization measures. At that time, nearly half of all sterilizations in the United States had been performed in California. This "Law on Preventing Hereditarily Ill Progeny" was also based on the American eugenicist Harry Laughlin's Model Eugenic Sterilization Law of 1922. Laughlin had "called for the sterilization of the mentally retarded, insane, criminal, epileptic, inebriate, diseased, blind, deaf, deformed, and economically dependent which included homeless and orphans."[43] Eventually, when the racial and anti-Semitic aspect of the Nazi measures were very clear and widely known, in the late 1930s, some supporters of the international eugenics movement started to distance themselves from Nazi racial hygienists. The Nuremberg laws were passed in 1935 and from 1937 the sterilization measures included ethnic and religious groups.

The Nazi pogrom of the 9-10 November 1938 and the numerous decrees limiting German Jews finally made some of the figures in the international eugenics movement uncomfortable.

Culture, nation and immigration

I want to go back quickly to the American Immigration Act of 1924 because it is one example of the relationship between race, nation, culture and immigration. It also shows how some other groups of people can be portrayed in order to justify their exclusion from the nation. Additionally, it highlights the distance we have traveled since the Enlightenment notion of common humanity and the original meaning of nation. Carl Degler argued that it was not the social scientists' interest in intelligence testing that created this act. The racial and ethnic basis for immigration was also not new. This act prevented all Chinese and Japanese people from entering the United States. But racist policies against Chinese and Japanese had already existed prior to the 1924 Act. Degler noted that the demand to curtail immigration had been increasing since the 1890s with labor unions' fear of economic competition and nativist groups' fear of the social character of the new immigrants. The new immigrants were from southern and eastern Europe and were "poor, Catholic, and Jewish, often illiterate, unskilled, and given to congregating in large cities, which were already seen as prone to crime, immorality, and violence."[44] The reasons underlying the American Immigration Act of 1924 were the racist attitude and hostility, particularly against Asian people, but also the demand for national unity and cultural homogeneity. Their hostility to Jews and Catholics was justified by a national need for social, cultural and racial cohesion. The hostility toward southern and eastern Europeans followed the nineteenth-century European sentiment where European cultures were defined against French hegemony by promoting the Nordic ethnic communities against southern ethnic groups. There was also, in the eugenics and racial science movement, a belief that immigrants with ancestry from the north of Europe were superior to those with Alpine or Mediterranean ancestry.

Another example showing hostility toward Catholics is the fear generated by the immigration of French-Canadian people, in late nineteenth century United States. They had come to work in New England cotton mills and thought themselves as American as anyone else but with simply their own culture which included Catholicism. Fear and hostility led to appalling living conditions and claims of an "invasion" of Catholics were loudly cried.[45] These kinds of racial, ethnic or cultural justifications as well as rationalization using the "economic competition" argument have, unfortunately, been applied many times and are still regularly used in order to restrict groups of immigrants. The nation is seen as a permanent, closed and fixed system rather than as a historical and transient concept susceptible to change with human actions. The perceived limit on jobs and resources is understood as the natural limit of this closed system and is fought over by different groups. But then, historically, there had been economic problems, depression or higher unemployment in nations with smaller populations than today's populations. The challenge for the radical left is to show that the limitations of resources are not caused by the presence or actions of groups such as immigrants today, or blacks and women in the past, but are the products of the particular economic system in which we currently live. Many discussions about race and racism also avoid the issue regarding the limitations of capitalism. The racial theories developed at the time when feudalism was overthrown, and capitalism was developing. The important question would be to analyze the specific social, political, economic and intellectual conditions that provided the space for the development of racial theories. What were the limitations of the new society that eventually gave rise to the anti-political reactions opposing the radical and revolutionary ideals of the

Enlightenment and the radical democratic impulse found in the nineteenth-century revolutions? The citizens of classical political theory were replaced by racial, cultural and national beings participating in the political world.

The meaning of citizenship today and the criteria for exclusion and inclusion in nations are not based on political definitions, in the classical political sense. After the recognition of a general lack of national direction and cohesion, discussions about values in Western nations have led to some soul searching. Some political positions, like laicity in France, have been redefined in order to justify the exclusion of others by classifying them with cultural and religious identities and with the imposition of authoritarian laws like the banning of scarves. The new wave of immigrants is one "tool" used to articulate new meanings for what it means to be French, American, German or British. In the West, at the end of the Cold War and at the end of the useful opposition one could use to define oneself, the ruling elites and those trying to promote their own particular nation have had many difficulties. In the past, claims such as "capitalism is better than communism," "western democracy is better than soviet communism" or "we are better than the Russians" had been useful in hiding the lack of positive visions and meanings. Today, immigrants or certain identity groups play a bigger role in order to hide the lack of positive meaning of what it means to be a member of a particular nation. Who are we? Are there any positive visions for the future, any positive and affirmative values and any principles that are collectively supported and practiced? Thus, turning toward immigrants and/or a particular section of the national population, like part of the working class, becomes an attempt to answer the question of what it means to be American, French or British. Immigrants or sections of the national population have the "wrong" religion, way of life, values, worldview or political opinions (for example, labeled as bigoted, racist or xenophobe) and the new meanings are defined as "not like them." Defining a nation with race in the Western world is no longer publicly acceptable in many nations since there are many minorities born and raised in the West who are part of the ruling elites and upper classes. Cultural differences, not racial differences, have become more useful in defining "us and them." The arguments against immigration, based on essentializing or racializing a particular group of people, need to be challenged and finally put to rest. It is an essential issue for anybody interested in opposing racism and racial divisions but also for those who are fighting against social inequalities and injustice and for the common interests of ordinary people. As Silverman has argued, the ambiguity between nationalism and racism have allowed many to hide their political position. He is, unfortunately, right to say that "anti-racism has frequently shared a similar discourse (or even the same discourse) as racism yet maintains its distance simply by cloaking itself in cultural nationalism as opposed to biological racism."[46] Contemporary anti-racism based on identities, for example, promotes racial thinking, race essentialism and increases the racialization of people.

It is important here to quickly highlight the difference between the idea of culture as human activity and the modern notion of culture used in concepts such as cultural relativism, cultural diversity, multiculturalism or cultural identity. Humans are social beings and so they always exhibit culture rather than simply existing as biological beings. Culture in that sense is specific to our species. It is related to our sociability, our human cognition and our mental abilities such as language and processes such as remembering, thinking or judging which allow us to understand the world around us, to gain knowledge and to transfer it to the newer generations, to organize ourselves in man-made communities. Culture in this sense can be also termed "civilization" and it is open-ended. The way "culture" is understood when applied to nation, ethnic group, communities or groups is no longer open-ended. We can see this when people talk about "saving their culture" as if there is something intrinsic, made by something other than humans as social beings, that needs to be saved *from* humans and their activity. These cultures are seen as different, separate and incapable of blending with others, with each individual bearing a very specific culture. This specific culture was given to them from birth or from ancestry. Discussions around family adoptions of children are places where these ideas can be expressed. The ethnic or national backgrounds of the children are supposed to matter in adoptions as if babies and young children carry their cultures with them or are representatives of specific cultures when going into a new family. Why would a child born in Sri Lanka and brought up in England have to learn about Sri Lankan culture as if it was his culture?

If people need to preserve a specific culture then they have little or no possibility to change themselves or the culture. This is associated with a perception that they have no possibility to fully comprehend other cultures that they have not inherited from their community or from their ancestry. Was the singer and songwriter Johnny Clegg, also known as the "white Zulu," unable to understand Zulu music and dance because he was born in the UK and was a white middle-class rather than a black migrant worker?[47] Apparently, people own specific cultures and others are not allowed to own it or use it as they want. "At its core, cultural appropriation is about ownership of one's culture," claimed Ijeoma Oluo. But then, she realized there is a bit of a problem with questions such as "who defines what is sacred to a culture?" and "who defines what is off limits?" So, she concluded that if one has enough respect for the marginalized culture then one will listen if an individual says that "it hurts me."[48] She is essentially saying that any individual from the "marginalized" cultures can, with a notion of harm, stop others from accessing, enjoying, sharing and engaging with these cultures. Authors from a specific cultural identity apparently cannot possibly understand, discuss or use characters with a different identity. If we follow Oluo's opinion, only a single individual would need to feel offended for a claim of cultural appropriation. This is, evidently, an important issue for novelists and some entered the conversation with more nuances.[49]

In our contemporary culture where claiming offense has become the way in which people make demands on others, it seems that cultural walls are built very high around individuals or groups of individuals. It is becoming increasingly difficult to climb them or destroy them in order to communicate with each other. Yes, we do have distinct habits, beliefs, norms, values, ways of life or traditions. It is fascinating to learn about how others live but it does not necessarily lead to the conclusion that this diversity of cultures is a barrier for us to understand each other, to change our ways and to stand together for a common good. With the focus on protecting cultural identities, we are again separated into discrete, immutable categories with their own characteristics. Possibilities for us to reach each other are very limited. Accepting and respecting our permanent differences without judging and having parallel lives with no few points of contact are increasingly seen as the natural way to live together. An anti-racism movement cannot be fighting for emancipation by promoting the idea that we are causally determined by race and/or culture with no room for reason, free will, solidarity and possibilities of acting together.

Hence, the continuity between "race" and "culture" is also the deterministic and fatalistic aspects of the two concepts. An early illustration of this was with French novelist and politician Maurice Barrès and the Dreyfus affair where a French Jewish captain, Alfred Dreyfus, was falsely accused and convicted of giving military secrets to the Germans. This is an example of the anti-Semitic notion, developed in the nineteenth century, portraying Jews as the racial or cultural enemy within the nation.

For Barrès, it did not matter whether Dreyfus was innocent or guilty because "nationalism requires us to judge everything with respect to France."[50] The important issue for him was not abstract justice but whether a specific verdict is beneficial to France. There is no truth or justice but French truth and French justice. Interestingly, his position also led him to be more "sympathetic" to Dreyfus than other people because he saw him as not responsible for his own thoughts and actions. "Here are ways of thinking and speaking apt to shock the French, but they are most natural for him; they are sincere, and we may call them innate," Barrès declared.[51]

As Tzvetan Todorov suggested, "culturalism" grows out of "classical racialism," replacing "physical race with linguistic, historical, or psychological race." Culturalism "shares certain features with its ancestor, but not all" declares Todorov reminding us of the later rejection of superiority and inferiority supplanted by a "glorification of difference."[52] Already with Barrès, we see that the notion of a single truth, single justice and more importantly the possibility for an objective understanding of the world is attacked. This is one fundamental distinction between racial thinking and culture relativism. One of the most prominent opponents of the Nazi racial theories was Franz Boas, professor of anthropology at Columbia University in New York. He is important for our discussion, and I will mention him later, because he is the key figure who introduced the concept of cultural relativism, which he coined, at the beginning of the twentieth century. This modern concept has been and is still constantly used by many groups to defend their political and social interests. The attacks on the idea of an objective world, promoted here by nineteenth-century nationalists, were seen long before the advance of post-modernism.

Dead-end anti-racism

There are numerous books such as *Why I'm No Longer Talking to*

White People About Race by Reni Eddo-Lodge or, *So You Want to Talk About Race* by Ijeoma Oluo which are written supposedly to let white people understand about "black experience." And this "black experience" seems to be often a very painful and dark experience. We are being told by Oluo that often "being a person of color in white-dominated society is like being in an abusive relationship with the world."[53] Discussing white privilege, an apparently "manipulative, suffocating blanket of power," Eddo-Lodge warned us that because "it's a many-headed hydra, you have to be careful about the white people you trust when it comes to discussing race and racism."[54] "It is about race if a person of color thinks it's about race," claimed Oluo, because "their racial identity is a part of them and it is interacting with the situation." An easy justification for racializing every single personal, social, political, economic issue one wants! You criticize my book? Well, it must be about race then.

Can white people understand black people? The answers are often in the negative even though there is a profitable industry with helpful people trying to explain cultural, mental, psychological differences between various ethnic groups. For sure, the presence of a profitable industry relating to a particular political issue is nothing unusual for our current society. There is also a profitable industry for those claiming to resist and fight "wokeness" or "social justice" for example. These discussions are much more prominent in the United States than in Europe for now, but possibly not for long considering the speed at which these concerns are propagated, even to places where people from diverse backgrounds are not as segregated as they are in the United States. The excessive concerns about "black" and "white" culture in the United States are due to the very segregated society where many black people and white people still do not live together. These racial divisions and segregations have created different communities with different cultures. Today, unfortunately, these cultures are often seen as impenetrable.

Even though biological racism seems less acceptable today, the divisions between cultures, the view of cultures as permanent and fixed, and the celebration of differences reproduce the same assumptions that underlie racial thinking and racism. The fact that some people in Europe, where there is much less segregation, import these ideas further demonstrates the underlying assumptions. What does black culture and white culture mean in a society where people grow up and mix with each other? I have used the political notion of "black" as I said in the introduction. A more specific example is the argument stating that Muslim cultures are barriers to people integrating to Western societies.

With the focus on individuality and identity, we are now divided into smaller and smaller groups. How can I, a person with a culture labeling me a French Afro-Caribbean, possibly understand and discuss African or Afro-American cultures and identities, let alone the culture and identity of a white polish man, a Jewish British man or a French Muslim woman? The common answer today is "no, I cannot really understand them, but I can accept and respect our differences without judging." Numerous social issues and problems, such as domestic violence, education and petty criminality are explained as problems of certain cultures.

The discussions around the issues of race, culture, nation and identity are based on specific understandings of the relationship between an individual and a group/community. Considering these philosophical questions which are not questions only for philosophers is essential when developing anti-racist ideas, politics and policies. I think the current perceptions underlying the issues of race and anti-racism, culture and identity are major barriers we need to overcome. In a way, I agree with Frantz Fanon when he argued that we do not have to "imitate Europe" who did not manage to act in accordance with its ideals but to recognize that "all the elements of a solution to the great problems of humanity have, at different times, existed in European thought."[55] We need to rediscover and further develop the best of humanity's understanding of itself and its ability to act. The best is, of course, not only European thought but it also cannot be simply rejected as "white thought." This is philistinism and anti-intellectualism, contemporary trends that are damaging to our public life. Europe had developed, in the past, many elements that would help us to move away from the stagnant intellectual water in which we find ourselves today. In the Enlightenment and during the age of revolution, there was a belief that human beings could shape their own destiny. This perception has nearly been lost today and replaced by a general sentiment that there is no alternative to the current society and that people simply have to be resilient in order to survive difficult conditions. This is seen with the current anti-racism movement with the endless discussions about white privilege, institutional racism, white supremacy, offense, systemic racism, diversity, representation, cultural appropriation, post-racial racism, color-blind racism, structural racism, multiculturalism, safe spaces, hate speech, microaggressions, individual responsibility, unconscious bias where all are based on the "grand ambition" of tinkering a little bit with the current system in order to make it better for a few more individuals of different backgrounds, living under difficult conditions. Concerns for poor black people are regularly mentioned but how many of these discussions look at solutions targeting economic inequality? There is no dispute here that it is important to try and make life better for individuals. I have great admiration for those who fight and help others, with better access to good education for example. The problem is when much of the anti-racism movement is reduced to tinkering, especially when this tinkering is only beneficial to individuals in the middle and upper classes.

Degraded universalism and multiple worlds

One of the important questions is how we ended up with this modern concept of culture so similar to the concept of race even though the idea of biological race seemed to have been mostly rejected. It seems there are no more attempts to express that, "I am human; and I think nothing that is human is alien to me/ Homo sum, humani nihil a me alienum puto." This very well-known quote comes from Publius Terentius Afer, known as Terence, a once-enslaved man, in the Roman Republic, who turned playwright. The radical meaning of this comment is lost for now. "*Nothing* that is human is alien to me," expresses a universalism that is foreign to many today. What is currently fashionable is a degraded form of universalism based on the idea that we, biological beings, are all from the same biological species called *Homo sapiens*. It is degraded because it suggests that the only universal qualities we have are biological in nature. It is related to the view that human nature or human essence can be defined simply by biology. And yet "Chimps aren't us," Jeremy Taylor demonstrated in his book *Not a Chimp: The Hunt to Find the Genes that Make us Human*.[56] Clinical neuroscientist and philosopher Raymond Tallis has spent most of his lifetime challenging scientism in order for us to have the intellectual space to fully understand human nature. As he notes in *Aping Mankind: Neuromania, Darwinitis and the Misrepresentation of Humanity*:

> The distinctive features of human beings – self-hood, free will, that collective space called the human world, the sense that we *lead* our lives rather than simply *live* them as organisms do – are being discarded as illusions by many, even by philosophers, who should think a little bit harder and question the glamour of science rather than succumbing to it.[57]

The authority of the natural sciences is constantly used in order to promote the notion that we are our bodies, denying our uniqueness and our past achievements.

Kenan Malik and others expressed very well an important shift we made when the concept of biological races was replaced by the idea of multiple and different cultures. In a simple way, we can say that the notion of "race" conceptualized human beings as biologically different and separate but living in a single common world, with common standards, laws and understanding but, more importantly, with the idea of an objective truth. One single world existed but various races were on lower parts of the ladder of social evolution and had not yet reached the top or simply did not have the ability to reach the best of this world. The understanding and interpretations of the world was singular and based on the supposedly superior race. The current notion of "culture," on the other hand, conceptualizes human beings as part of one common biological humanity with equal mental capabilities but separated into distinct cultures with distinct understandings, interpretations, values and worldviews. The possibility for an objective truth and objective understanding has disappeared. We went from "one world with many races to one race in many worlds."[58] This is a very important shift with a lot of consequences for liberation movements. Theorists of the concept of culture have reworked some of the assumptions underlying racial theories but have also moved away from the essential notion of objective truth and objective knowledge. "Your truth is not my truth" or "white people truth is not black people truth" are expressions of this important shift. It is worth recalling some of the figures and events that led to this important change.

Franz Boas is a key figure

Franz Boas is a key figure for our current concept of culture. He is considered the father of cultural anthropology. He was born in

Germany in 1858. He studied what was called "psychophysics," wanting to understand "how the characteristics of the observer determined the perception of physical phenomena." His studies focused on analyzing the way Inuit perceived the color of seawater. As Kenan Malik noted, the letter Franz Boas wrote after meeting the Inuit or "savages," as he called them, expresses his belief well:

> I often ask myself what advantages our "good society" possesses over that of the "savages." The more I see of their customs, the more I realise that we have no right to look down on them. Where amongst our people would you find such hospitality?...We have no right to blame them for their forms and superstitions which may seem ridiculous to us. We "highly educated people" are much worse, relatively speaking...As a thinking person, for me the most important result of this trip lies in the strengthening of my point of view that the idea of a "cultured" person is merely relative and that a person's worth should be judged by his *Herzensbildung* (noblesse of heart).[59]

He believed in "equality" and challenged scientific racism but his position was to argue for an equality in differences. "Savages" and Westerners are not the same but the two groups are equal. This is familiar because this is the usual argument today when people argue for equality. The Enlightenment philosophers believed that, with progress, divisions they saw as artificial would disappear. Boas acknowledged diversities as permanent but saw all groups with equal value. His notion of cultural relativism stated that people from a specific culture could not criticize the cultures of others. But we can also see with this letter that his beliefs arose from a dissatisfaction with his own society.[60] He was not happy with the social and political situation in Germany. Some think him being a Jew may have contributed to his sense of alienation from what was happening in Germany. There was also a general sense of pessimism throughout Western society at the time. He eventually emigrated to the United States 6 years after finishing his doctorate.[61]

Boas had a great influence on anthropology but also on the issue of race. His concept of culture was seen as a direct challenge to the idea that differences in mental and social abilities were due to race. This was a time of strong official segregation in the United States. His best-known work, *The Mind of Primitive Man*, published in 1911, argued that the mental capabilities of "savages" did not differ from those of civilized people, challenging the still common belief that the concept of social evolution could explain the social and intellectual inferiority of the primitive people. His other influential contribution is his argument that our theories and ideas were not from our own reason but from the influences of our ancestors and of our environment.[62] Boas revisited the old German romantic view of culture I discussed earlier, when I talked about Herder and others, but he abandoned the idea of hierarchy between culture. Humans are separated by different cultures, each of these cultures "is the outcome of its geographical and historical surroundings." Denying the existence of a universal standard to judge other cultures, he argued that "civilization is not something absolute, but that it is relative, and that our ideas and conceptions are true only so far as our civilization goes."[63] For Boas, "culture was synonymous not so much with conscious activity as with unconscious tradition" noted Kenan Malik.[64] He relied on culture and history rather than on biology to explain an individual's behavior, ultimately forgot reason and moral conscience. His position led him to say that "we cannot remodel, without serious emotional resistance, any of the fundamental lines of thought and action which are determined by our early education, and which form the subconscious basis of all our activities."[65] Thus, an individual is unlikely to change but, in addition, it is necessary for the individual to keep his particular culture.

Anthropologists began to think that the study of humanity involved the study of all different cultures. Boas encouraged his students to study all ethnic groups including the main culture in the United States. Many of his students became important anthropologists who developed some of his ideas but also managed to make anthropology an important academic discipline. They legitimized and popularized the idea of culture. Alfred L. Kroeber, Robert H. Lowie, Edward Sapir, Melville Herskovits, Ruth Benedict and Margaret Mead are some of his students who made their own important impact in the field of anthropology but also in our knowledge of the world and of ourselves.

UNESCO and culture

After the Second World War, the United Nations was founded with the official purpose of promoting international cooperation, preventing further conflicts, promoting social progress and support for the fundamental human rights. It is easy to forget the history of human rights when it is frequently discussed as if the notion had always existed but that it had simply not been applied properly in the past. As Kirsten Sellars remarked, the ideal of human rights is not timeless or eternal but was developed during the Enlightenment. She gave a very interesting account of the people, diplomacy, campaigns and pragmatism that led us to the rise of human rights after World War 2.[66] Promoting the ideal as eternal has allowed restrictions on reasonable and valid criticisms against human rights policies which, nonetheless, are very influential in our political and social lives. The very fact that this has such a significant effect on our political and social life should have been reason enough to develop a thorough and continuous debate about the pros and cons of this ideal.

The impact of anthropologists such as Boas and his students was clearly seen after the Second World War. After the war, members of the United Nations decided to create a special branch, UNESCO (United Nations Educational Scientific and Cultural Organisation), under the directorship of biologist Julian Huxley, which would deal with questions concerning science and culture. They wanted to draw a line between the past associated with war and ignorance and the peaceful present connected with knowledge. The Allies had fought the war using as defense the idea that they were fighting against tyranny, racism and ignorance. Western scientific racism had become a big problem with its connection with Nazism and the Holocaust. After the systematic discrimination and annihilation of millions of people justified with racial and eugenics theories, many people started to see the race issue as a destructive force in society. The Jews had been persistently persecuted throughout the ages but the notion of a "semitic" race was fully developed in the nineteenth century during the development of racial thinking. Thus, UNESCO claimed in its constitution that "the great and terrible war that has now ended was a war made possible by the denial of the democratic principles of the dignity, equality and mutual respect of men, and by the propagation, in their place, through ignorance and prejudice, of the doctrine of the inequality of men and races."[67] It is worth highlighting these few words again: *"propagation,* in their place, *through ignorance* and *prejudice."* We have seen above and in the previous chapter how racial theories were developed. I discussed a few of the intellectuals, scientists and other educated men who developed these ideas, the historical contexts for their development and some of the applications of these theories in politics and policies. Racial theories did not develop and propagate because of ignorance and prejudice. Nonetheless, in *The Race Concept: Results of an Inquiry,* published in 1952 by UNESCO, scientists argued that, until the 1920s, race prejudice "only affected areas on the margin of civilization, or continents other than" the European continent.[68] Trying to distance themselves from the Western history of racial thinking, they claimed it was "the outcome of a fundamentally anti-rational system of thought" in "conflict with the whole humanist tradition of our civilization."[69] It is true that racial doctrine opposes the humanist tradition but it is also a product of Western intellectual tradition, the tradition that challenged Enlightenment ideals.

After the war, UNESCO started to promote the notion that racism was the result of an individual's ignorance and behavior. The United Nations Economic and Social Council asked UNESCO to consider "initiating and recommending the general adoption of a programme of disseminating scientific facts designed to remove what is generally known as racial prejudice."[70] Individual psychology and irrationality are the source for the problems of racism according to UNESCO which stated that "knowledge of the truth does not always help emotional attitudes that draw their real strength from the subconscious or from factors beside the real issue."[71] This definition of racism as an individual's racial prejudice will later have considerable consequences on the fight against racism, with blame placed on the wrong and often the more powerless people.

Racial science versus anti-racist science

To build their program of education, UNESCO had invited a team of cultural anthropologists and sociologists, under the leadership of the British-born American anthropologist and renowned anti-racist Ashley Montagu. Anthropology and sociology fields of studies, at the time, were already moving toward the idea of culture rather than race because of the consequences of Nazi applications of racial theories. They agreed that all men belonged to the same biological species, that "national, religious, geographic, linguistic and cultural groups do not necessarily coincide with racial groups" and that it would be better "to drop the term 'race' altogether and speak of *ethnic groups*." Humanity was still classified into three major dynamic divisions which changed throughout history: The Mongoloid, Negroid and Causasoid divisions.[72] Thus, they agreed with the concept of biological races understood as groups separated by a specific variation in certain genes but disagreed with the notion that biological differences determine social and cultural differences. There are no doubts about a biological variation within humanity but the important issue is always to ask why certain variations become socially meaningful and labeled "race" or "ethnic group" while others do not matter.

In accordance with the belief that racism can be fought with an educational program, they noted that one common human trait "which above all others has been at a premium in the evolution of men's mental characters has been educability, plasticity" and that all "are capable of learning to share a common life."[73] This plasticity of mind and education now defines the post-war "cultural man" and can, together with social and cultural differences, explain the variation in human behavior and mental characteristics. Whenever one wants to promote a political or social issue today, one seems to go into demands for more "education." Apparently, there is increasing need to educate people: about their health, about the need to stop eating certain food groups, about the number of hours they need to sleep, about the appropriate behavior when faced with persons belonging to a different culture, about the right way to speak to a child, about the time needed to spend with your pet, about the appropriate way to build an intimate relationship, about diversity and equality or about the right political opinion one needs to have to be considered a morally superior individual. More "education" is seen as the way to change the world. But what does it really say? The belief in "plasticity" is the belief that human beings can be manipulated to support an idea rather than the need to convince them and make them rationally recognize the idea as right or good. The human mind is seen as plastic, malleable; therefore "education," which usually mean assertions, statements, propaganda or images or words to guilt-trip, will make people know the right ideas they should be supporting. It is based on a very degraded view of other people and usually ordinary people. People need to be "educated" as if they were young kids at school rather than be convinced as if they were adults with rational arguments. Their ability to reason is denied with the promotion of mental plasticity.

The idea that people needed to be educated with the right ideas rather than convinced with rational arguments became very widely accepted in liberal democracies. The contempt for people's ability to reason is not new and is also certainly not unique to left identity politics as some would like us to believe today. John Carey, in his book *The Intellectuals and The Masses: Pride and Prejudice among the Literary Intelligentsia, 1880-1939*, argued that many "founders of modern European culture" show contempt for the rapidly growing population of ordinary people, in the late nineteenth and early twentieth centuries. He looked at the reaction these intellectuals express, through their writing, against the "masses." When education meant access to humanity's knowledge, many were not happy with ordinary people getting into it. In England, the "difference between the nineteenth-century mob and the twentieth-century mass" was "literacy" and fear and contempt were the reactions to this change. The educational legislation at the end of the nineteenth century, the increased literacy of the working class and the development of newspapers catering for the lower classes provoked a hostile reaction from many European intellectuals.[74] Education which develops knowledgeable, intellectually autonomous and critical individuals is much more dangerous for those who want control and order than "education" that teaches individuals to behave and think in specific and restricted manners.

The first team of anthropologists and sociologists invited by UNESCO provoked an outcry. Geneticists and physical anthropologists were upset because they had not been invited to join the first team. A second team which included eminent biologists such as Theodosius Dobzhansky and JBS Haldane was formed. They concluded that "available scientific knowledge provides no basis for believing that the groups of mankind differ in their innate capacity for intellectual and emotional development."[75] Naturally, this particular conclusion created a few reservations among other scientists. Racial science had been supported by many before the war. What is interesting to note is that between the time in the 1930s where many still supported aspects of racial theories and 1946, with the UNESCO declaration, not much evidence had developed and yet many scientists had changed their minds.[76] We can see how politics, not science, had promoted but then later seemed to reject the idea of race. UNESCO was trying to use the authority of science to support its statements the same way racists had been using science to give authority to their racial theories.

Scientists can provide evidence for one political side or the other but, of course, interpretations of results will always be contested by other scientists. There is an objective world and objective truth. Science is a human activity which has been extremely useful in improving humanity's understanding of the natural world. We see the progress in science when we use our knowledge of the natural laws for our benefits. Medicine is a good example. And yet, our potential for progress also means that a contemporary scientific truth is not eternal. It will change when our knowledge of the objective world develops further. But the essential point here is that race and racism are not scientific issues but political, social, philosophical and moral issues. Human biological diversity is a scientific issue but race is not a scientific category. Have you ever heard of a scientific definition of race? Ask one person claiming the existence of biological races to define them scientifically for you and you will end up with fuzzy, evasive explanations that have nothing to do with science but completely rely on popular perceptions.

With our eyes, we see biological differences between individuals and recognize that some groups have darker skin than others for example. But a human perception is not a scientific definition. Our human perception will tell us there is silence somewhere and yet our dog will hear noises he will interact with. A "black" person, if considering ancestry as definition, can have a skin color ranging anywhere from white to dark brown. But then, how was ancestry itself defined? Which section of one's ancestry was chosen to define one as "black" or "white?" Science does not give us all the answers to our moral, political or philosophical questions.

The development of racial theories was in response to the continuous social inequalities in the new capitalist society despite the belief that social transformations from feudalism to capitalism will eventually erase inequalities, divisions and differences. The, still existing, inequalities were consequently interpreted as natural and permanent. The developing fields in science had provided the means to justify the belief in natural differences and hierarchy between groups of people. It is not science which will give us the answer as to how we want to see ourselves and others. Biological differences between people have always existed and there is nothing wrong in recognizing these differences. After our first holidays together, in the French West Indies, my husband and I had laughed at how my light brown skin had become so much darker under the sun while his white skin had stayed as white as ever with little patches of red where he had not been careful enough. Nothing in his physical appearance gave a clue to the fact that he had just spent more than 2 weeks under the tropical sun. We actually enjoy our biological distinctions in many ways, and also our cultural differences but the most important aspects of our lives are the common interests, values and principles that we share to build our life together. Thus, these differences have only meanings, good or bad, when human beings and/or society give them meanings. The meanings my husband and I put behind them are certainly not related to the notions of "oppressor" and "oppressed." Activists who describe racism as systemic white privilege or as the original sin have divided people into two immutable categories: the oppressors and the oppressed, showing their underlying mistrust in reason and autonomy.

Still, my husband and I cannot deny the existence of racial identities and the social content of these identities. Through the individuals, we can "see" society and to be "black" or "white" is simply not like choosing to be a meat-eater or a vegan. Racial identities are not personal lifestyle identities. They do not depend on personal tastes or preferences. We do not have to treat each other differently in our personal lives to recognize the social content of the current racial divisions. Several groups have been and are currently racialized. These groups are not always the same at various times and places, but the borders created by racialization are not built by choice. These racializations have created divisions between different sections of society and they cannot simply be dismissed. These divisions are not natural, are not inevitable but are social and real. Claiming that we are all the same, despite our biological differences, has a tendency to ignore the fundamental divisions that exist in society. It creates a vision that society is simply an aggregate of individuals with their interpersonal relationships. It means that, somehow, if I look at my husband as equal to me, and if we all do the same, all will be well. This is forgetting the fundamental structure of society and the important relationships between the individual and the producing society. We cannot grasp human life without considering the relationships between humans, society and nature. The relationship between humans and nature, the act of transforming nature in order for us to fulfill our needs, is fundamental to our human existence. The transformation is done through our labor or productive activity. All human societies must produce to survive but each society or stage of production will have specific forms of the forces and social relations of production needed to organize production. The form that the division of labor takes is specific to a particular society. The specific forms that they take in a capitalist society compared to a feudal society, for example, need to be considered and understood because they define the historically specific relationships between the individuals and society. The social laws are independent of our will but the forms they take are historically specific, i.e. transient. Social relations are not simply interpersonal or cultural relationships as it is often understood today. Society has to be understood in its totality in order for us to understand our important social divisions. And as far as I can see, Karl Marx has done the best job so far. Thus, the social position of different groups of people need to be analyzed in order to understand the reasons for the social inequalities they have to deal with. Their specific positions are not due to individuals' responsibility or the group's culture.

Races are social categories developed through history, through the development of our understanding of ourselves and of our ability to act in the world and through our struggles and social development. Mark Fisher maintained that a moral critique of society, simply highlighting the suffering people experience, "only reinforces capitalist realism" in the sense that these forms of suffering start to be seen as an "inevitable part of reality."[77] I suppose "life is unfair" is one very common way people dismiss any hope for change. We are supposed to do our "little bit" every day and make ourselves better for people around us but when big questions, such as the worldwide social inequality between the different classes, are asked, any solutions proposed are automatically seen as utopian. Fisher is right when he explained that for an ideological position to become successful, such as the current notion that healthcare or education "should be run as business," it must first become naturalized. And yes, the notions of permanent racial and cultural divisions have been naturalized.

Race and culture essentialism, the view that people belonging to different races, ethnic groups or cultures have intrinsically different characters, dispositions and ways of thinking, has become a common worldwide view. Hence, like other radical theorists, Mark Fisher argued that "emancipatory politics must always destroy the appearance of a 'natural order,' must reveal what is presented as necessary and inevitable to be a mere contingency, just as it must make what was previously deemed to be impossible seem attainable."[78] Right now, the current anti-racism movement is not destroying the appearance of a natural order but reinforcing it, with the help of those in power today. It is not a coincidence that a commitment to diversity and representation and a focus on identity, for example, are championed by many among the social, economic and political elites who have personal interests in keeping the social order.

Racial thinking has not been overcome yet and now some of the anti-racist ideas are promoting it. It is not surprising then that racial science is still supported by some people. Asking for their motivations behind their continuous support is quite revealing because it shows the pessimistic view they have about people. We know that facts have meanings only after interpretations made by humans. How racists and anti-racists interpret differences between groups of people depends on what they think are important questions to answer and on what they think of human beings, society and the world. The underlying pessimistic, anti-human and anti-political views of racial thinking and cultural relativism are what needs to be confronted. Therefore, I think it wrong and unproductive to try and ban this racial science. We often say in scientific research that "absence of evidence is not evidence of absence" and that is a justification used for the continuous search for a scientific definition of race. There are an infinite number of scientific issues, thus a simple question would be to ask about their desperate need to discover inequalities between biological groups. No need to ban. Arguments against racial science are numerous but supporting academic freedom and free speech is essential. As John Stuart Mill argued in the nineteenth century: "All silencing of discussion is an assumption of infallibility" and none of us are perfect.[79]

Separated by cultures

UNESCO had a big influence in the popularization of the idea that cultures were the main forces that determine and shape human beings. The promotion of cultural relativism, originally developed by Boas and his students but further developed by others such as structuralist Claude Lévi-Strauss, popularized the notion that humanity is separated into numerous cultures that can only be understood using norms, ideas, values and concepts found within each of these cultures. No hierarchy between cultures is possible because they cannot be judged with universal human notions. Boas had developed his concept of culture as a challenge to racial hierarchy and racism and had promoted the notion of equality. Human beings are shaped and molded by their specific cultures without any possibilities for them to reason and change. Reason, the basis for our autonomy and moral conscience, is denied with a vision of human beings as simple representations or owners of specific cultures. The anti-human sentiment and anti-humanist attitude are found both in cultural relativism and racial thinking.

For these reasons, I think multiculturalism and diversity *policies* need to be opposed. Unfortunately, the distinction between multiculturalism and diversity as facts of life and as lived experiences and, multiculturalism and diversity as policies is often completely blurred. This blurring can then lead to arguments denouncing the presence of too many people of different cultural backgrounds. Not wanting to have too many Chinese people in your home town or wanting to restrict the Muslim population in a specific area are obviously racist or xenophobic opinions. Rejecting others because of their various backgrounds, these opinions express an opposition to human diversity as a lived experience, as a fact of life. In fact, this is often argued on the grounds of protecting one's culture or the interests of one's race. Those who argued this are the mirror image of the supporters of multiculturalism and diversity policies. Multiculturalism is about protecting cultures; these cultures are grasped as if they are out of the control of the human beings currently alive and simply imposed upon them. Culture, in these cases, is no more the way people have decided to live today. It is not the norms, habits, traditions, ideas, beliefs and ways of life they want to keep but the norms, traditions and ways of life given to them by their ancestors. They are portrayed as custodians of culture developed by ancestors. The resulting effect is fixed cultures, prevented from changing by policies and self-proclaimed cultural gatekeepers. American culture, for example, with this definition, is not what people in the United States do, the norms, values, and habits they have decided to adopt today but a fixed culture of the past people are supposed to follow and preserve.

In the next chapter, I will briefly look at identity and identity politics. The contemporary focus on identity is due to the change in the cultural and intellectual perceptions of the individual. It is because of the continuous role and importance of politicized identities in society. I will argue that the first politicized identities were the racial and national identities developed in the nineteenth century. But the defeat of all radical and universalist politics in the mid-twentieth century has made social movements and radical activists turn to identity politics. Left-wing politics rejected universalism and developed the politics of difference where differences in culture and identities are celebrated. This celebration of differences and the politicization of identities within the current therapeutic culture has created what many understand as "identity politics." The focus on more and more fractional identities is the result of our current social, economic and cultural circumstances. A lack of meaning in a world which seems out of control, a perception of the individual as isolated, vulnerable and threatened by all others and an anti-humanist portrayal of human beings as unable to act on the world have created a search inward. The old anti-political trend is accelerating. Identity politics is not just from the left and liberals but is accepted and used widely. The difference is in the identities supported. In fact, politics today is understood only through identity politics even though identity politics is anti-political at its core.

Chapter 3

Identity and Identity Politics

The notion that black identity or blackness was created and imposed by white people and by the Western elites was replaced by the belief that black people are not simply passive victims defined by others. They could determine their own culture, community and identity. Their self-defined identities promoted positive self-images and were seen as acts of liberation from the oppressive atmosphere of white society. Today, we encounter all kinds of racial, social and cultural identities celebrating differences between distinct and immutable groups. These identities are still seen as positive self-images but are often based on the notion of survivors proudly dealing with hatred and trauma. The identities are based on claims of oppression and discrimination with the sense that the wider society is hostile to the specific identity group. The feelings from members of these identities who apparently have survived and are still surviving terrible circumstances often define the identity of the group. The definition of these identity groups is dependent on the reception of their particular demands by the wider society to recognize their suffering and to accept what would make life better and easier for members of these particular groups. In essence, the wider society is seen as the threatening enemy of a particular identity but, at the same time, with demands for recognition and privileges, as the solution to their particular problems.

The politicization of these numerous identities is what creates identity politics. Unfortunately, most opponents of identity politics have a very narrow understanding of it. It is mostly understood as a new politics coming from the left, liberals and progressives in response to perceived social injustice, oppression and discrimination suffered by sections of the population. Many accounts of identity politics mention the Institute of Social Research commonly known as the Frankfurt School, the radical movements of the sixties, and the exhaustion of liberalism at the end of the Cold War and the rise of neoliberalism. In the previous two chapters, I discussed why some of the ideas underlying contemporary identitarian anti-racism are obstacles preventing us from confronting racial divisions and racism. Contemporary understanding of race, and the celebration of cultural differences, cement the status quo and deny the possibility for social transformation. There are many authoritarian consequences of identity politics such as increased support for censorship, restrictions on the possibility for autonomy and moral conscience, further atomization of society and increased mistrust of the others. They are discussed constantly by those claiming to oppose identity politics. Rather than concentrating on arguing against these consequences, I want to discuss how the narrow approach of understanding identity politics today is hiding the fundamental issues that need to be addressed in order for us to effectively oppose identity politics and develop new ideas for a socially, economically and politically better world.

Broader meaning of identity politics

First, I believe that identity politics is not politics in the classical meaning of politics. It is based on social, cultural and personal identities politicized to enter the political realm in order to advocate for particular interests and political demands. These political demands are done with the notion that society as a whole is the enemy to each particular identity group. I have tried to emphasize the anti-political nature of both race and culture when the classical notion of "citizen" is replaced by racial, cultural or other social identities. These politicized identities are destroying the classical political notion of citizenship and so damaging an important part of our human world, the political world, thought to be first developed by ancient Greece. The political world is where we people with various understandings of the world and of ourselves can reach each other through reason and convince others of the correctness of our ideas, decisions and actions. If we insist all ideas are determined by identities, if we cannot transcend identities through the exercise of our reason, then there is no room for collective action and solidarity with others.

If we understand identity politics with the concept of "politicized identities," then we have to admit that identity politics did not first develop in the twentieth century but as reactions against eighteenth-century American and French revolutions, Enlightenment ideals and radical democracy. Identity politics first developed at a time when the notion of democracy as "demos" and "kratos" or "power/rule of the people" and political definition of citizenship were rejected by the Western elites in the nineteenth century. The first social identities, which became politicized, were race and nationality with the development of the national character. We saw in the previous chapter that the nation was quickly defined not as a political and voluntary association of citizens but as a community defined by race, blood, ethnicity and/or culture (including history, ancestry, traditions). As we will see later, the earliest meaning of "identity" has developed into several other modern meanings during the twentieth century, especially in the second half of the century. Hence, the earliest politicized identities were not based on the same definitions of identity and of the self as the ones we have today. The past and present identities are, however, all *social identities* that are politicized to enter the political realm. There is both a continuity in the politicization process and an alteration in the content of these identities. The modern meanings of identities and the various manners in which the self is understood developed at specific political, cultural, intellectual and social circumstances which are very distinct from the nineteenth-century circumstances. Therefore, the differential meanings of identity lead to differences in the way identity politics presents itself.

The resulting politicized identities through various historical times were not influenced by the same understanding of the individual or the same cultural atmosphere. The nineteenth-century elites had started to understand the world through biological race and their identity was mediated through this. Their own understanding of who they were was still very much defined by their position in the social hierarchy. It was not seen as an individual decision. They believed their social position was determined at birth and by their race. The modern form of identity politics developed in the second half of the twentieth century arose in an increasingly atomized and individualistic society, where social positions were not seen as determined by birth and where a therapeutic culture, fostering a sense of vulnerability, was progressing. Today, the sense of self is perceived as isolated from the whole of society, alienated, vulnerable, in need of guidance by experts and in need of protection from the others. Thus, the notions of the individual and the sense of self have changed. The fragmented identities today are defined by a hierarchy of victimhood, oppression and vulnerability. The inner self represented by these identities has changed but to see identity politics as new prevents us from seeing the fundamental problems politicized social identities create in society.

The abstract idea of equality together with the reality of social inequality and social divisions were rationalized into racial and cultural divisions. This understanding further entrenched social divisions and made them look natural and permanent for the wider population. These racial, cultural and national identities are expressions of *social* and *economic inequalities* but are used in the political world as if they are the equivalent of the classical political notion of "equal citizen." In reality, individuals and groups do not have equal political power. The big political inequalities are mainly due to the numerous inequalities in the social, economic and cultural worlds. But the real roots of social divisions and economic inequalities, found in this particular capitalist system of production and social organization, are no longer visible because they have become simply represented as details and characteristics defining politicized identities. The important social contents of some of these identities are hidden away as simply qualities of individuals who demand help from the wider society. Identity politics hide the real basis of political, social and economic inequalities. A working-class black woman is simply an individual with distinct attributes compared to an upper-class white man. These two individuals will be seen as having distinct interests simply because of the differences in identities. They do not have the same political demands but the reasons for their differences in interests are naturalized and thus become hidden from political questioning. Identity politics keeps the status quo and prevents us from analyzing, questioning, discussing and confronting the most fundamental issues that need to be addressed. Identity politics has been and still is a useful tool for those wanting to keep the status quo because it completely obscures the foundations of the capitalist social system.

Of course, with its support of racial identities, identity politics does not oppose racial thinking. The roots of the social divisions created and reproduced spontaneously by the capitalist mode of production were hidden by the ideology of racial thinking. This ideology fixed the divisions through a racial line and racial identities were created. The differences between the lower and upper classes became a "black and white" issue for example and race came to be part of our reality. These new identities are seen as the expression of humanity's will, as if the original social divisions are the creations of human nature and humanity's conscious actions. They are not. Throughout history, various types of societies, for instance the pastoral, the agricultural, the feudal or the capitalist societies, are based on distinct modes of production. They have their own forms of social laws and social divisions, but also various social identities, independent of the will of humanity.

Moreover, contemporary identity politics with its numerous fragmented identities promotes the notion that all of these identities can be understood and considered in the same way. Racial, cultural, national and sex identities, which have meaningful social contents, are put at the same level as lifestyle identities. It creates a tendency where identities are believed to be created by personal choices, tastes and preferences. The real social division between men and women, created by the need for society to reproduce itself, and which takes a historically specific form in the capitalist system, is increasingly seen as simply a problem of conscious human behavior and individual choices. Apparently, one can simply choose one's sex identities between man and woman or create new ones.

Even though contemporary identity politics challenges liberal rights, civil liberties and, contrary to liberalism, promotes equality (of outcome) above individual liberty, it still follows some of the liberal understandings of the individual and society. It celebrates the individual and promotes the idea that individuals can be fully free without society. Through the existence of social pressure, society is seen as a barrier to individuals' full development. And it is based on the notion that society is simply a collection of individuals with interpersonal and cultural relationships. This is not correct. There is an important contradiction in capitalism. The individual is celebrated and developed while the need for others, for society is essential for the individual's development. The divisions of labor and the increase in labor productivity, in our current system, have allowed for the possibility of free time away from the necessary labor needed for survival. If we look at the very poor places where people still have to produce most of their needs themselves, most of their time is spent in activities which simply permit them to survive and not develop as individuals with their own hobbies, talents and preferences. The capitalist mode of production has opened up the space for the potential of individuals' full development. What Karl Marx had realized is that the development of the capitalist system will also create obstacles preventing the further development of individuals' full potential. Thus, capitalism is a step up from feudalism but it eventually limits humanity's social development. The cooperative nature of the mode of production of the capitalist system and the increase in labor productivity have freed the individuals from necessary survival activities. The division of labor and cooperative nature in capitalism is seen in the fact that several advanced capitalist nations are now centered around services and financial services rather than productive labor. However, the need we have of others for us to have a better life, where we can spend more time in intellectual, artistic and other pleasurable activities, is counter-posed by the competition within the capitalist market. We fight for jobs and resources against each other within this system. Others are seen as competitors and enemies. Liberalism has tried to reconcile or hide the social divisions created by the current mode of production by celebrating the individual and by naturalizing the forces of production. It created a society seen only as a collective of individuals, who do not have the important social aspects of their lives recognized, but who are bound by society's institutions, norms, interpersonal and cultural relationships. Identity politics does not oppose this view and thus cannot promote the notion of social transformation, of radically changing society's mode of production in order to oppose capitalist social inequalities. In fact, we can see that those supporting identity politics have become purely moralistic and have abandoned politics and discussions of the material conditions of our lives.

I have made a lot of assertions here. Proper arguments need to be developed. I will look at some of them in this chapter but I hope to be able to carry on the conversation in the future. I believe that the current focus on criticizing left identity politics only builds arguments that leave the fundamental problems of all identity politics untouched. It also creates a tribal atmosphere witnessed by those involved in political discussions, where different tribes attack each other without questioning the status quo and the notion of TINA (There Is No Alternative) we have lived under for decades. Moreover, the focus on left identity politics by those claiming to oppose identity politics helps to keep alive the conservative and liberal belief that social inequalities and social problems are mainly due to individual behavior and responsibility. The myth of meritocracy, for example, is used as a counter-argument to demands for representation.

Identity

The question "who am I?" is not a new question but a philosophical question that has been asked and answered in many different ways throughout history, since the birth of the individual. But the concern for identity that has become a preoccupation throughout Western countries in recent years is not just asking this question. Identity has become one of those popular words taken for granted, used in all kinds of public discussions and in many different contexts. It seems to be a word that does not need explanations or definitions. Identity plays a very important role in many academic disciplines and in popular conversations. The concerns and questions of identity are now seen as if they have always been there, as if they have always been part of the general conversations until one looks at the relationship between identity, identity politics and politics or at the relationship between the individual and society.

The word identity is not a new word in the everyday English, French (identité) or German (identität) language, although it had a more technical, mathematical meaning in the French and German language, according to Gerald Izenberg.[1] However, it was not really used in academic, professional and political fields until the twentieth century. In his history of identity, Philip Gleason mentioned that the original *Encyclopedia of the Social Sciences*, published in 1936, had no entry for "identity." Identity became only a concern for the social sciences in the 1950s and appeared for the first time in the 1968 edition.[2] Whether the word was used by some people in the past or not, what is important to note is that the meaning of identity in the past, which is still also in use today, has developed into new meanings. Interestingly, even though the term had changed and became important in many aspects of our lives, the definition of identity found in the *Oxford English Dictionary* in 1983 still only reflected the old meaning of sameness. The dictionary defined it as follows: "The sameness of a person or thing at all times or in all circumstances; the condition or fact that a person or thing is itself and not something else; individuality, personality."[3] In the past, identity was about defining who we are as a person in the sense of sameness or the same self. Our civil data such as names, birth dates or parents' names were a way of describing our identity, to prove that we are the right person talking to others at a particular time.

This particular meaning of personal identity has also been important since the time of John Locke, for people discussing the philosophical problem of the unity of the self, of the relationship between mind and body.[4] This particular discussion is still very much on our minds. Are we the same person if we download our mind into an artificial intelligence? If we clone ourselves, how would we define the clones? Which identity will these clones have? Will the clones still be me? The older meaning is still in use with, for another example, the concerns for stolen identity when one uses your data without your permission.

The modern concept of identity has been influenced by and developed through different academic disciplines and intellectual trends such as psychology, social sciences, anthropology. Existentialists, such as Jean-Paul Sartre and Simone de Beauvoir, with their development of the concept of the "Other" and belief that identity needs to be overcome, have shaped the discussions. The attempt to reject it by postmodernist intellectuals who were anti-essentialist and the introduction of the concept in social movements by political activists have further developed the concept.[5]

Marie Moran, in her book *Identity and Capitalism*, divided the contemporary meanings of identity into three categories: the "legal," the "personal" and the "social" sense of identity. The "legal" sense of identity, as in "identity card," is mostly about proving who you are. The meaning behind this is generally not new. The "personal" sense of identity uses psychological and physical characteristics to define the core quality of an individual, the content of selfhood. These characteristics define what makes an individual's inner self unique, different from others. The contemporary notion that one needs to discover one's true self suggests that the core quality can be given by God or nature, not created or chosen by the individual defining himself. But there is also a common perception that the sense of self can be chosen with the current lifestyle identities. More importantly, the personal identity is often defined by active recognition and differentiation. People are expressing their personal identities by choosing a specific way of life or adhering to a fashion in order to mark their inner selves as dissimilar to others.[6]

It is understood that the personal identity has first originated from the concept of "identity crisis," an expression first coined by Erik Erikson. A psychoanalyst working with World War Two veterans and children, he used his clinical experience to develop his concepts of identity and identity crisis. This psychological conceptualization of identity, using Freudian concepts, understood identity as part of the normal human development. He was interested in psychological well-being and tried to understand what he called "identity crisis." He thought that war veterans suffering from what used to be called "battle fatigue" suffer, in fact, from "identity crisis" because they had lost their previous sense of who they were after their experiences of war. His interest was focused on personal identity that he understood as both social and psychological. Identity was the sense of knowing oneself through the interaction between "the core of the individual" developing and the society in which the child is developing into adulthood. The child will first only identify with the parents and their values (no judgment) but growing up, he will accept and reject what he used to only identify with and develop his identity. Identity was seen as a dynamic process with a certain sense of individual autonomy and it developed after identification. Erikson was concerned about the pathology (identity crisis) observed in some children that he believed was due to the rapidly changing environment found in the modern world. For Erikson, the psychic problems come from social problems.[7]

He popularized the idea of identity with his work and his books. His first book, *Childhood and Society*, was published in 1950. But then, he finally disagreed and struggled with the changes in the concept when it was introduced and developed in other academic disciplines. For example, he disagreed with the introduction of the notion of self-conception and self-image.[8]

Some of the main explanations for why identity became such an issue in the twentieth century, for both academia and the general public, point to the problems of modernity, World War One destruction of previously accepted traditional identities such as the "gentleman" identity, consumerism and mass society, conformity, changes in social classes, individualism, and, of course, the enormous success of psychology as a new subject in academia, in politics and in public life. Modernity was seen as creating an isolated individual, obsessed with consumerism in a fast-changing and chaotic society. The concept of identity has become a useful and easy go-to analytical tool for those concerned about the relationship between individual and society and for those discussing social problems.

Erik Erikson argued that "we begin to conceptualize matters of identity at the very time in history when they become a problem."[9] He thought it useful to develop the concept because it helped us understand some aspects of ourselves but also could help to deal with some particular issues newly arising. Psychology has become the tool used in many aspects of our lives today. As Eva Moskowitz noted, "problems that were once considered political, economic, or educational are today found to be psychological."[10] She was discussing the United States, arguing that the tendency to look at the mind for explanations and solutions developed from the mid-nineteenth century. Psychological explanations have become very common throughout the Western world, not just the United States. Agreeing with the philosopher Ian Hacking's point, Patrick Bracken argued that:

> Increasingly, Western societies understand the impact of violence and other types of suffering and formulated questions about responsibility and morality through the sciences of memory and psychology. Most non-Western societies deal with these issues very differently, most often through a mixture of religious, spiritual and political ideas and practices.[11]

Thus, psychological explanations for personal or social problems are not universal and yet they are used to explain social, economic and political problems worldwide. What Bracken is concerned about is the need to look at contexts to understand how individuals will view a particular event and react to it. He is opposing the ideas that "the mind exists as separate from, and in relation to, an outside world" that lead to the notion that life meanings are internal, found in the "interior" mind.[12] People, from distinct cultures and moral frameworks, do not view and react to similar events, such as bombings, in the same ways. Human beings are rational and social beings. What one finds offensive will depend on one's individual past experiences and one's ideas and opinions. This is why the constant claims of "offense" or "outrage" by individuals these days cannot be taken as claims representing the whole group. Unfortunately, the ideas Bracken is opposing are currently widely supported. They are influential in the contemporary need to define and redefine personal identities and the demands for these identities to be recognized by the wider society.

The modern meanings of identities which represent as well as cause the increasing focus on the individual inner self degrade our relationship with others. First, society is seen as an enemy an individual has to free herself from. Social pressures, institutions, norms and people around the individual are seen as obstacles to her self-expression. The trans activists today represent this well when they argue that transgender people have to free themselves from the norms and social pressures that prevent them from changing gender or choosing a new gender. The demand is for society to retreat and leave the space for individuals to express themselves as they wish. How one individual *feels* becomes more crucial in conversations about change than how people, including the individual, *think* and rationally argue.

The third contemporary sense of identity discussed by Moran is the "social" sense. She argued that social identity seems to mean "claiming membership" of a given social group. In fact, when looking at ideas such as the claims of multiple identities by proponents of intersectionality, it is clear that a social identity is the social group itself and that it is not necessarily associated with the "experience of being a member" of the group.[13] When one claims, "as a black woman, I think that...," one is saying that the ensuing expressed thought is dependent on the crossing of the social group "black people" and the social group "women" in one particular individual. The opinion is supposed to be the product of the intersection between the black identity and the women identity. Social groups, including social classes, are treated as identities. This is why we can have academics, journalists, entrepreneurs or politicians claiming to be "working class" despite the fact that their economic and social position put them in the middle class, capitalist class or as part of the ruling elites. Moran made a more crucial point when she noted that "though identity is treated most commonly as a substantive property of individuals and groups, in fact, identity is a classificatory device, that classifies according to what is considered essential to a particular person, type of person, or group." Thus, identity "is an essentializing mechanism." The concept, including its past and present meanings, is *itself* an essentialist concept because "it is premised fundamentally on the notions of sameness, oneness and how these constitute – or are essential to – a given entity."[14] Specific characteristics (physical, cultural, psychological, moral or intellectual) are defined as essential to the individual or group, common to all members of the group and different from all other individuals or groups. These definitions are usually not created internally within the group but by self-appointed community leaders and gatekeepers of identity groups. Is he a real Muslim if he has an opinion that is not accepted by self-proclaimed community leaders? Who decides whether a special artifact is part of the culture defining an identity group and thus belongs to that group?

The process of categorizing people into essentializing identities defined by specific characteristics that are seen as essential for the particular category reduces the liberty of individuals and groups. It demands conformity as well. If an individual wants to see himself as black, he is forced to follow the norms and rules of the identity group, otherwise he is seen as "unauthentic" or "non-black." The identity classification denies individual agency. It prevents individuals from expressing their own self, own individuality.

The modern concept of identity is certainly no more

liberating than the concepts of race and culture. They are all essentialist ways of "construing personhood and grouphood" which leave no room for reason, free will and moral conscience. Individuals are simply determined by fixed identities. But denying our individual agency is dangerous. Conscience and moral judgment are exercised at an individual level. If we lose the habit of using our individual conscience to make decisions and act upon those decisions, we lose our moral autonomy, our ability to decide what is right and what is wrong and can act in ways that are very immoral. The German Nazi leader and one of the major organizers of the Holocaust, Otto Adolf Eichmann, is an important example of what can happen when a person refuses to think for himself, to use his conscience and to make moral judgments. His actions did not originate in his hatred of the Jews and Gypsies even though he was an anti-Semite. His excuses were that there were no voices in Europe which opposed Nazi policies and awoke his conscience and that he was doing his duties as a law-abiding citizen. Hannah Arendt, with her famous book *Eichmann in Jerusalem: A Report on the Banality of Evil*, has stressed well the importance of individual moral judgment even in the conditions where there is a moral collapse around the individual who needs to decide what is right and wrong.[15] Making moral judgment means then to accept individual responsibility for one's decisions and actions. Eichmann refused to take responsibility for his horrendous decisions and actions. In our modern Western society, with a focus on fixed identities that are seen to causally determine our decisions and actions, individual responsibility is easy to ignore. Claims that "his religion made him murder people" or that "his white identity made him support racist ideas" deny individual responsibility. If people are not responsible, how can we blame them for their decisions and actions?

Politicized identities

The modern meanings of identity reframed some older concerns such as the issue of the inner self and the relationship between individuals and society but what Moran had argued is that the concept itself is an essentialist mechanism that divides people into categories. She is right but I think that race, culture and nationality had started to play this role in the nineteenth century before the development of the modern meanings of identity in the twentieth century. Identity is currently based on a definition of the inner self as weak, vulnerable, isolated and threatened by society. In the past, the inner self had anchors and links with families, communities, institutions, social clubs and political parties. Much of these pre-political attachments have diminished and the individual lives in a more atomized society even though he still needs others to survive. Furthermore, the individual is generally seen today more as an object than a subject. Thus, race, culture and nationality in the past were based on distinct conceptions of the self within historically specific social and economic circumstances but they were already essentialist mechanisms.

The politicization of social identities is not a new phenomenon. Racial, cultural and national identities were used in the political realm to argue particular positions, since the nineteenth century. The national character, which became "national identity" later, is often based on the notion of sameness as if the national population is uniform within the nation and different from other populations. It is also based on the notion of "ipseity," i.e. selfhood or identity, related to the perception of continuity and stability between past and present.[16] The nation has its own distinct identity like a person and the members of that nation are part of that identity or represent this particular national identity. Nationality became an essential part of an individual, defining his behavior and mental characteristics. Race, developed in the nineteenth century as seen in the first chapter, was a very

125

important aspect of Western elites' identity. It was used to base their political positions and demands both within their nation and abroad. These early identity politics were certainly not based on inclusion. The identities may have represented bigger groups than the ones today but they were excluding many people while fighting to satisfy only particular interests and privileges. In fact, Sarah Churchwell went further with the point in her article "America's Original Identity Politics" when she argued that "the United States was founded on identity politics," if one considers "*The Economist*'s description: political positions based on ethnicity, race, sexuality, and religion."[17] We can add gender as another identity used in politics. But the observation that identity politics developed before the twentieth century does not lead to the conclusion that all politics is identity politics as many try to maintain. Not all politics is about arguing for the interests of a group against the interests and common good of the wider society.

And this highlights the big tragedy of contemporary identity politics: those with universalist political positions, with demands for equality for all, equal opportunity and better life for all have given up on their universalist positions to imitate the dividing identity politics that originated from the right, from those opposing the Revolutionary Enlightenment ideals. The notion that politicized identities can be useful for groups to fight for their particular interests has been accepted by radical activists and groups fighting against racism, for justice and for equality. But by using politicized identities, they have reinforced the notion of permanent and natural divisions based on race, ethnicity and culture. They have also strengthened the notion that race, ethnicity, culture and identity determine our fate. Challenging racism using politicized racial identities does not challenge racial thinking. In fact, it promotes racial thinking as a progressive step either by celebrating perceived racial differences or by racializing others. Because others have been racialized, there is now a demand for white people to also recognize they are members of the white race or whiteness. The current "unracialized identity" of white people becomes a problem for the anti-racist activists because, according to them, whites do not recognize the significance of race without recognizing themselves as members of a racial group.[18] It is true that all of us partly use our personal experiences to interpret the world and thus those who have never considered other people's lives or do not want to access humanity's knowledge on the issue of race and racism will simply ignore the problems. But the solution given by some anti-racist activists is actually to racialize white people as well, rather than really oppose the concept of race. "Let's all recognize we are from different races" has become the "anti-racism" call of today. This is the justification of contemporary anti-racism in promoting racial thinking. Radical activists started to use politicized identities and racial thinking when they gave up on the possibilities of social transformation and solidarity with others who were needed to achieve, collectively, this social transformation. The wider population became the problem for those supporting these new anti-racism ideas. The interests of "marginalized" groups were no longer to change society in order to make it better for all but to fight for their little corners within the current society.

But the more crucial point is that politicized identities prevent us from opposing the social, economic and political inequalities meant to be the targets. The social and material basis that created these different "marginalized" groups is no longer opposed. With the politicized identities and identity politics, the real sources of social divisions have simply become specific and essential characteristics defining particular identity groups. A worker is seen as part of the working-class identity group with specific traditions and cultures. These traditions and cultures are no longer understood as dependent on the material conditions of their lives and the social and economic inequalities suffered by the working class can be ignored.

We can start, like Marx, and recognize the fact that human beings need to produce in order to live and satisfy their physical needs. But to satisfy these needs, humans will inevitably, through their productive activities, create new "non-physical" needs which will then also become necessary in order to satisfy the original physical needs. Thus, we can say that the foundation of human existence and all human activities and needs originate in the sphere of material production but are also mediated and take forms in different ways. As István Mészáros noted:

> Productive activity is, therefore, the mediator in the "subject-object relationship" between man and nature. A mediator that enables man to lead a human mode of existence, ensuring that he does not fall back into nature, does not dissolve himself within the "object."[19]

Productive activity, essential for human existence, creates more needs and increases the complexity of human social organization. This activity also allows the possibility for humanity to control nature and to gradually free itself from nature's domination.[20] This means that we have to look at the foundation of human existence and understand the specific forms it takes in the capitalist society in order to understand the basis of the social and economic inequalities we experience today. If the expressions of human society and its economic structure are simply acknowledged as features, definitions, identities or labels of individuals and groups, the roots that led to the creations of these various and divided groups are ignored. Individuals and groups, like the white working class, with no power and no responsibility for the way society is organized, end up being blamed for social problems. In the *Preface to a Contribution to the Critique of Political Economy*, Karl Marx argued that:

In the social production of their life, men enter into definite relations that are indispensable and independent of their will, relations of production which correspond to a definite stage of development of their material productive forces. The sum total of these relations of production constitutes the economic structure of society, the real foundation, on which rises a legal and political superstructure, and to which correspond definite forms of social consciousness. The mode of production of material life conditions the social, political and intellectual life process in general. It is not the consciousness of men that determines their being, but, on the contrary, their social being that determines their consciousness.[21]

The white working class or even white people as a group are not guilty or responsible for the economic structure. But "the legal, political, religious, aesthetic or philosophic – in short, ideological forms in which men become conscious of this conflict and fight it out"[22] should be explained, defended and opposed with a good grasp of the material condition of life. At the moment, anti-racism and radical ideas are only developed through interpreting our cultural life, interpersonal relationships or ideological forms.

The important meaning of social justice has been destroyed. The opposition to economic and social inequalities has been replaced by demands for cultural recognition and a celebration of difference. A few handouts and patronizing state protection for identity groups portrayed as vulnerable victims who, apparently, cannot deal with words and images are declared "social justice." How can one ever take seriously anti-racist ideas which claim to care for black people, who are suffering from social and economic inequalities, but which propose solutions such as increased diversity, more representation and celebration of black culture? All discussions which would lead toward hard questioning of the material basis of social division are avoided. Identity politics have been a useful tool for this and this is why it has become so pervasive.

Shelby Steele clearly highlighted the changes in expectations, between anti-racist politics at the time of the civil rights movement which still had a certain universalist ambition, and anti-racism politics where identities have become the basis for political demands: "In the age of racism I had wanted freedom as an individual; in the age of white guilt I was learning to want power as a black."[23] Political activists today seem to think that the only way to engage is through a vicious competition between racial identities. The most important aspect of our selves is denied; the identity as a political agent.

Post Second World War and anti-Enlightenment

The war, with the systematic extermination of millions of people and the Nazi experiments in concentration camps, led to demands for new visions of society. Wars would be prevented with the development of science and technology, and racism would disappear through education. But the post-war relief, even in the radical and social movements, did not lead to an increased support for Enlightenment ideals such as perfectibility, progress, universalism and the importance of human reason. Radicals later rejected the idea of universalism to promote a politics of difference where each group could claim distinct cultures, values, morals, identities and these differences were celebrated. They explained social problems and social divisions with race, culture and identity, imitating other political ideologies which had incorporated anti-Enlightenment ideas.

There was an optimism for what science and technology could do for people's everyday lives and for humanity in general. John Gillott and Manjit Kumar, in their book *Science and the Retreat from Reason*, argued that "until the late 1960s, science was generally regarded as laying the basis for progressive interventions in a natural world viewed as threatening, capricious, and potentially destructive."[24] But the important point is that post-war enthusiasm for science was already based on the belief in human beings' limitations. Enlightenment belief in science was supported by the belief in humanity's ability to rationally understand humans, society and nature. It was also supported by the belief in progress, human development and human perfectibility. The philosophers believed that progress comes from the use of reason, from challenging prejudices, norms and traditions of the past and by creating new ideas and paths for the current society. Science, as a rational human activity, was seen as an important tool for progress. This was not the common belief after the war despite the enthusiasm for science. As Gillott and Kumar noted: "the post-war reception of Karl Popper's ideas shows the Western theorists recoiled from the idea of bending nature, through science, to human will." Popper opposed the "assumption of an *objective reality that human beings can understand.*" For him, science could not recognize the Truth. A scientific interpretation can only be shown as false but not proven true. This view results in undermining the idea of progress in scientific knowledge.[25] In fact, Gillott and Kumar went further and argued that nineteenth-century intellectuals had already broken the link "between the advance of natural science and the advance of human happiness," "between science and reason, between science and progress" with, for example, Auguste Comte's positivism and John Stuart Mill's utilitarianism.[26]

We cannot achieve any social progress without increasing our understanding of the objective world and of nature and without the bending of nature to create a new social reality. Of course, this is not the same as supporting the current irrational destruction of the natural and social world we observe in some parts of the world today. Natural laws are independent of humanity's will and they cannot be transformed or destroyed but they can be understood and used for humanity's own benefits. We do not destroy the law of gravity by flying a plane. Planes are designed to overcome the force of gravity. Humanity has a need to interact with nature in order to survive and reproduce. In earlier societies, natural laws dominated humanity more than they do today. Our understanding of plant and animal breeding and the advance in agriculture are examples of our progress. We became less dominated by natural laws. These natural laws, mediated by different historically specific societies, are expressed as social laws influenced by humanity's increasing understanding and control of nature. Social laws are independent of individuals' will. But one of Karl Marx's important contributions in our understanding of the world was to show that these social laws can be understood and analyzed scientifically, that they take different forms in various societies and that they are "specific to the particular stage of development of society."[27] Our need to interact with the natural world in order for us to eat and survive, for example, takes a social form. Every human society studied will show a need "to work, produce and consume in order to reproduce itself." But, as Frank Furedi observed, "the forms in which labour is organized – as slavery, serfdom, the peasant economy, wage labour – are historically specific, governed by the special laws arising from particular relations of production."[28] When people with environmentalist or romantic ideas maintain that they do not want us to bend or control nature for our benefits, they are effectively arguing an anti-progress and anti-human position where nature completely dominates humanity. Let's remind ourselves what nature can mean; females of some animal species such as primates kill their own offspring or other young in order to give others a chance to live. Resource competition, scarcity, need for protection against aggression are some of the reasons for these actions. There is currently too much of a romantic notion associated with nature. These females are limited by what nature produces while human society can and did develop an understanding of nature to produce more for more people. Agriculture is a good example where we produce more with less manual work to feed more people. The time and labor needed to produce food are reduced and can be used for other new needs such as spending time in movie theaters with the family. It is not a humanist, Marxist or pre-war left-wing tradition to try and stop economic progress, to demand de-growth or to demand a downscaling of production and consumption. It is based on a perception of limitations humanity is expected to adhere to and to accept and thus it is a reactionary anti-human idea. It can also be linked with racism when poorer countries are asked to stop their own economic and social development in order to "save the environment."

Contest between "individualist Man" of Liberalism and "socialist Man" of Stalinism?

The new modern meanings of identity were developed after World War 2 during the contest between liberalism and communism. Kyriakides and Torres argued that the anti-Enlightenment position, which had developed from the shock of the Second World War and the Holocaust, was given free rein at the end of the Cold War, when the contest between the "socialist Man" of Stalinist Soviet Union and the "individualist Man" of Western liberal democracies ended. A weak version of Enlightenment Man was fought over by liberalism and socialism/communism but at the end of the Cold War and the fall of Stalinist Soviet Union, "individualist" Man left standing could not sustain the weak version of Man. The anti-Enlightenment views of humanity were able to gain credence again at the end of the contest.[29] Both "individualist Man" and "socialist Man" were weak versions of the Enlightenment definition of humanity. In fact, the authors argued that, "The West's optimism of the individual will did not exist as an internal pre-supposition of the liberalism; rather, it reflected the political imperative of countering the alternative Enlightenment model of human beings – the collective subject – of Soviet communism."[30]

Liberalism developed from the reactions against Enlightenment, the French and the American revolutions in the eighteenth century, the rights of Man[31] and later, the revolutions of 1848. It was later on influenced by John Rawls and his theory of justice based on post-war social democracy. Post-war socialism/communism progressed from Stalinism and the failure of the Russian Revolution. It also grew from Western critiques of Marx's theories developed after the failure of working-class and left-wing movements. Optimistic and future-oriented humanism and universalism had been rejected on both sides. But liberalism and communism as well as conservatism did provide ideologies with different understandings of the world, of the individual and society and thus provided distinct solutions to social problems. These ideologies do not exist as distinct anymore in a very depoliticized Western world.

We have seen that the development and introduction of racial thinking in Western understanding of society and of human beings contradicts the humanism and universalism of the Enlightenment. The alternative thought to be found in culture rather than race was also shown to be against the Enlightenment notion of human beings. Nations, which incorporated race and culture in an attempt to build their national identity and cohesion, also developed a general anti-Enlightenment view of society and humanity. Widely supported eugenics thinking, based on the belief that reaching a certain perfection in human beings is equivalent to progress, led to attempts to exterminate whole groups of people seen as undesirable. This belief in perfection is the opposite of the notion of perfectibility in Enlightenment thinking. But, of course, not all theories and viewpoints of the world incorporated racial thinking, cultural fatalism or other anti-Enlightenment models of human beings. The end of the Cold War did have an influence on our current view of humanity. The "victory" of liberal democracies over the Soviet Union models did not lead to celebration for the liberal "individualist" Man and celebration of capitalism as a good social system. What the end of the Cold War has shown are the many weaknesses in liberalism and the lack of positive arguments in support of the current capitalist system.

I do not argue that all Enlightenment thinking was good, all liberal ideas are reactionary, and all ideas of Marx must be followed. I am arguing that some of the best thoughts in humanity's understanding of itself, society and nature have been abandoned rather than developed further. Ideas are not the only important forces shaping history, but they are critical. Humanity, in its struggle to survive and create a better world for itself, has come a long way but it still has much to do in order to develop the full potential of individuals. It is not the time to look at our belly button, protect it from harm and stress while admiring it as if it can give us meaning and direction.

The "individualist" Man and liberalism

The "individualist Man" was not the "Enlightenment Man" but "limited Man." It may seem strange that liberalism is discussed here but I think that the liberal ideology is not a solution for the fight against racism. It supports the status quo and with some of its ideas it becomes a barrier to a movement aiming to transcend racial and social divisions and transform society in order to create a new one. Sheldon S Wolin argued in his book *Politics and Vision: Continuity and Innovation in Western Political Thought* that liberalism has been mischaracterized in the twentieth century because democratic radicalism and liberalism are grouped together despite them being two "distinct traditions of political thought."[32] George Sabine agreed and noted that "between the philosophy of natural rights in the Revolutionary Era and the liberalism of the nineteenth century there was a profound difference of temper and spirit. The philosophy of natural rights was in essence a revolutionary creed."[33] Wolin viewed democratic radicalism as only partly influenced by John

Locke, an English philosopher and one of the most influential of the seventeenth-century thinkers, also known as the "Father of Liberalism." Democratic radicalism is, in fact, mostly originated from "eighteen-century rationalism and the experience of the French Revolution."[34] In contrast, Lockean liberalism is influenced by pre-French Revolution, by John Locke but more importantly by classics economics and philosophers such as David Hume and Adam Smith. The anti-Enlightenment thoughts of David Hume, for example, can be seen in his understanding of knowledge. He proposed that knowledge cannot come from experience and observation. Thus, by concluding that no belief comes from reason he, in essence, put a strong limit on reason.[35] Wolin interpreted the difference between Lockean liberalism and the radical democratic tradition as a divergence in the belief of "the ability of human mind to fathom reality and to translate the results into practical actions."[36] The term "liberalism," argued Jonathan Israel, is a "general historiographical disaster" when used to describe the earlier intellectual and political trends in the nineteenth century. This term generally lumped together "anti-democratic moderates, heirs of the "moderate Enlightenment" and post-1800 philosophical radicals conserving the Radical Enlightenment legacy."[37] It may be useful, for those promoting liberalism in their war against contemporary neoliberalism and left identity politics, to claim it as heir to Enlightenment and radical democratic tradition but this is a myth.

Thus, early liberalism developed as a reaction to democratic radicalism and its ideals were the expression of the outlook of the new capitalist class in the nineteenth century. The capitalist class became increasingly powerful socially and economically. The development of liberalism allowed them to have more political power. Their outlook turned away from the rationalism of the Enlightenment and the natural rights of the revolutions. Romanticism, idealism, utilitarianism developed to replace the more revolutionary concepts of the Enlightenment. The increase in political power, with the widespread support for their ideals such as the "greatest happiness principle," happened before the new working class had started to organize themselves in a new labor movement with their own ideology.[38] One of the efforts of liberalism was to develop concepts of government which would give as much freedom as possible to the capitalist class to act without the interference of the state. The underlying liberal idea justifying this position on liberty was that nobody can really know another's true interests. This idea, of course, does not question the differences in economic, social and political power between the social classes.

The liberal concept is actually based on the notion of an abstract individual based on the characteristics of an individual from the capitalist class, an individual with much social, economic and political power already. The concept of freedom currently accepted today was developed from this. We understand liberty as freedom from state interference or freedom resulting from restraints on state power to intervene in our lives. Our current concept sees freedom as absence of interference. But there is an older and more important meaning; the ability to exercise control over our own lives or freedom as having *power against interference* has been largely forgotten. The difference between the two freedoms can be understood this way: one can choose what to eat only by choosing something on a specific menu given by another (freedom as non-interference) or one can go out and eat whatever one wants without being forced to choose on that particular menu or with having the power to refuse the specific menu and to choose another (freedom as non-domination). In his book *Just Freedom: a Moral Compass for a Complex World*, Philip Pettit discussed the way the original meaning of freedom as non-domination developed in the Roman Republic and was maintained until the new meaning developed with the liberal utilitarian philosopher Jeremy Bentham in the early nineteenth century.[39] I think the change between the two meanings really shows the beauty and power of a rational argument well-made and the consequences when it is not intellectually and politically challenged. According to Pettit, Bentham wanted to extend freedom to women and workers and thus "argued that freedom requires just the absence of actual interference, i.e. free rein, not the absence of a power of interference. This made it possible to maintain that women and workers could be free, provided their masters did not actually misuse their power of interference."[40] Bentham managed to develop a notion of freedom with less depth, less significance, less value in order to extend it to others. Women and workers have finally freedom to live within the social system where they are exploited without having to consider the possibility of a "freedom" from exploitation and from domination by other human beings. This new notion went well with the newly developed capitalist society where workers' lack of control over their lives and the domination by the capitalist class did not concern the state as long as workers could be free to enter into a work contract. Slaves or serfs were not free to enter into these contracts but workers in capitalist society have the "choice."

Humans described as liberal subjects are seen as rational, rights-bearing individuals, autonomous, able to make their own decisions for their own lives. This can only be accepted as truth if the real barriers blocking people from exercising their own reason, autonomy and control are forgotten, like today. Many of the "anti-capitalist" talks do not target capitalism as a transient system that needs to be understood and changed if need be but as a permanent way of life where excesses affecting some people should simply be curbed. Moral issues such as the terrible conditions of life of very poor people are what animates these talks and the solutions are simply to relieve the terrible conditions rather than oppose the material reasons that led to the existence of "poor people" and "non-poor people" in the first place.

Early *laissez faire* liberalism, giving the capitalist class free rein, was later opposed by the developing labor movement. In its later development, liberalism tried to reconcile the capitalist and the working class and their opposing interests in order to become the main ideology in Western democracies. It attacked the most brutal aspects of capitalism and the effects of the capitalist class pursuing their own interests.[41] The revolutions of 1848-49 and the later upheavals had a big impact on liberalism because claims from the working class could not be ignored any longer. With more political and civil liberties, liberal thoughts tried to portray a society where the divisions between social classes were no longer important. Liberalism, after World War Two, promoted the notion of racism as a problem of individuals' psychology and behavior rather than it being a social problem, for example. Subsequently, the solutions proposed were education and policies to regulate and control the relationship between the different races. The view that race could be transcended through collective human actions and profound social transformation was not considered.

One of the points of this book is that race, culture and identity are based on the denial of human rationality and thus humanity's potential in understanding and acting upon itself and the world. Anti-racist ideas based on a similar view of humanity are barriers preventing us from challenging and transcending race and racial divisions. Liberalism is also based on a view of human beings where reason is not understood as central to humanity as seen earlier with the break between science and reason. The importance of reason is also undermined when reason is understood as meaning the opposite of "stupidity" or when it is seen as the agent itself, as the element deciding and acting on behalf of humanity rather than seeing rational human beings as the agents. The liberal subject as a "rational man" is a myth if we understand reason as the ability which gives humanity the potential to understand the world, to convince others and to act collectively in order to change themselves and the world around them.

From early on, liberalism had seen passion, desire and feelings as the key to moral judgments, decisions and actions. The liberal notion of the "greatest happiness" principle is based on this. Liberals saw reason as simply there to determine "the most efficient means to achieving the ends proposed by feeling."[42] Jeremy Bentham, a key figure in liberalism, central member of the "Philosophical Radicals" group and the founder of utilitarianism, put happiness at the heart of his moral code. "It is the greatest happiness of the greatest number that is the measure of right and wrong," Bentham believed.[43] He introduced a psychological and subjective definition into politics. But what is happiness? Were the slaves happy with their lives because they played music and danced? An argument I heard many times when I was young. Bentham thought that what mattered "was the *consequence* of any act. What determined the moral character of such consequences was the principle of utility." Utility for Bentham meant the "capacity to engender happiness, both in the individual and in society."[44] He had developed the first consequentialist theory. Consequentialist theories are still very important in our thinking with questions such as "will the results of a policy be justice or equality?" Consequentialist theories are not concerned with important questions such as "what is the motive behind the new definition of freedom?" With liberalism, the common good is no longer the product of reason but rooted in desire, in values based on a certain understanding of pain and pleasure. In the economy, human beings' willingness to satisfy their own self desires were seen as the basis for the common good. Later on, the suggestion that the happiness of future generations should also be considered was added to liberal theories.[45]

In the second half of the twentieth century, in 1971, when the liberal consensus was already failing, John Rawls published his book *A Theory of Justice* which had and still has an enormous influence on liberal political philosophy and its critics, on modern liberalism and on current social justice theories. The context for his theories, known as "liberal egalitarianism," was political and social circumstances that had already disappeared. These were the post-war boom, social democracy, liberal democracy and an emphasis on welfare and regulatory state where social problems were dealt with through expert policies and a big administration. His ideas were built on his theory of "justice as fairness" and the belief that fulfilling self-interests were the key to people's actions. In his thought experiment, he argued that if people had to agree with a society, unseen behind a "veil of ignorance" and where they would not know the position they would occupy in the new chosen society, they would choose a society where the worse-off people live as well as possible (in case they ended up as part of the worse-off group). He is following the liberal conception that fulfilling self-interests and desires is the key to governance. And yet, in real life, we can hear of many actions people take, including the sacrifice of their own health or life to help others.

Rawls's just society follows two principles: "a principle of liberty, which affirms citizens' basic rights and freedoms, and of equality, which calls for inequalities to be limited and resources arranged so that they benefit the least well-off members of society."[46] His emphasis was on redistribution of resources to alleviate some inequalities suffered by the worse-off persons but he still accepted that inequalities were inherent to society. Thus, inequalities do not need to be confronted but managed. In essence, he only argued against the excesses of capitalism. Some inequalities are even justified if they lead to advantages for all. This is how affirmative action can be justified for example. To achieve redistribution, institutional solutions were emphasized with the help of a highly centralized, technocratic and autonomous state possessing the "power to redress the socio-economic inequalities" without having to examine the "political economy of concentrated wealth and corporate power."[47] Rawls's political liberalism "was based on a deliberative vision of politics that saw democracy as modelled on discussion" and other older concerns such as "nature of the state, political control, collective action" were squeezed out of political thought development.[48]

One of the important alternatives to the liberal egalitarianism was the school of thought known as communitarianism. It originated with Michael Sandel's book *Liberalism and the Limits of Justice* published in 1982. Sandel took issue with the atomistic, non-socially linked liberal individual Rawls is portraying when he used the thought experiment. Individuals cannot simply get out of their social and personal experiences and thus, cannot be behind a "veil of ignorance" when choosing a just society. Sandel advocated for community to be prioritized over the individual because "(c)ommunity describes not just what they have as fellow citizens but also what they are, not a relationship they choose but an attachment they discover, not merely an attribute but a constituent of their identity."[49]

An important point here is that, in liberal egalitarianism, the protection of political rights and civil liberties takes priority over opposing economic inequalities. The protection of rights and liberties is done by the state which has become technocratic and autonomous. With the rise of neoliberal policies such as privatizing part of the welfare state and public institutions and with the anti-democratic transnational institutions, even these rights and liberties are threatened.

I am discussing liberalism here because some who opposed identity-based anti-racism are calling for liberalism and liberal values to be supported. I think it is clear that I do not see this as a solution. The important point here is to note that the radical and revolutionary aspects of Enlightenment thinking were attenuated or rejected by liberalism. It is difficult to claim liberalism today as a source of ideas which will help us to radically transform society and challenge racism because the basis of the liberal ideology is to hide the important differences between the capitalist and working classes. It is worth remembering the consequences of ideas on our consciousness, decisions and actions. The descriptions we use to understand the world are also part of our world, of our reality. A liberal view of the world will create a different reality to a conservative or a communist view. The categories such as race or class, concepts such as identity, culture and rights are used to describe what we understand the world to be in reality but they also shape reality and become part of our reality. This means that ideas can also distort our understanding of the objective world, of the world external to us.

For example, the development of the race category and the continuous acceptance of this notion are some of the beliefs that have twisted our understanding of the capitalist system. The opinion supporting notions of permanent racial divisions between people is the basis of contemporary perceptions of racism as the "original sin" white people are presumed to be born with or as a lack of understanding of racial relations. The current perceptions of racism are also based on the view that it is a problem of an individual's behavior or psychology. Hence, solutions proposed will tend to be demands to control individuals' behavior. Cultural expressions of racism will be targeted with discussions about education or access to state provision. Many contemporary anti-racist ideas help to keep the status quo in the sense that these solutions do not challenge the foundations of the social system. Their focus is on the ideological and cultural expressions of racism such as racial discrimination, stereotypes, prejudices and racist policies rather than analyzing the link between racial inequality and social divisions that the capitalist production creates. We have seen in the first chapter how social inequality became understood as racial inequality. The foundations of our current system have been naturalized, taken for granted and are seen as permanent features of all human societies. If one believes that the current system is the only possible solution for a human world, then one's solutions will be to change within the system without ever questioning the system itself. A lack of political imagination and extremely low expectations are major obstacles today.

The "socialist Man" and Stalinism

The "socialist Man" of Stalinist Soviet Union was certainly not "Enlightenment Man." In fact, Stalinism in the Soviet Union moved far from the Enlightenment, from Karl Marx's thoughts and theories and from Marxism developed at the end of the nineteenth and beginning of the twentieth centuries. The high point of classical Marxism ended in 1924 when Lenin died, after the failure of the 1917 Russian Revolution and of the European, in particular German, working-class uprisings in 1918-20. The First World War had already broken up Marxist theorists between the social chauvinists who supported their own nations and those opposing the war and the support for the ruling elites.[50] The Enlightenment's radical and revolutionary ideas were ignored, attenuated or destroyed by mainstream counter-revolutionary reactions. The radical and revolutionary ideas found in Marxism were progressively taken out and destroyed, mainly by those claiming to be proponents of Marx's ideas. Marxism very quickly degraded with the advance of Stalinism in the Soviet Union. Stalin took over after the death of Lenin, increasingly purging all opponents such as Trotsky, Ryazanov, Bukharin and Preobrazhensky.[51] The Soviet bureaucracy readily created dogma out of Marxism to help in their justification for their own existence and to claim support for themselves. The disintegration of the working class, the development of the new bureaucracy repressing and controlling the working class, the absence of economic and social cohesion, the lack of basic rights and liberties in the Soviet Union cannot be ignored. The "socialist Man" of Stalinist Soviet Union had moved backward, away from any concepts of rational and social human beings, perfectibility, progress and development of humanity's potentials, universalism or freedom. It was the "chronic weakness and instability of the capitalist world order" that helped the Soviet Union survive for so long. Frank Furedi concluded that:

(I)ts transformation into a superpower owes little to any inherent drive within the Soviet social formation. The stagnation of Soviet society reveals its failure to evolve a developmental dynamic. From the point of view of historical materialism, it is necessary to conclude that the Soviet Union contains no progressive tendencies. Its very survival owes more to rivalries among the imperialists powers than to its form of social organisation.[52]

The propaganda from the Soviet bureaucracy claiming the positive development of individuals working hard and sacrificing themselves for the benefit of the whole society could have been easily set aside if the contest between the capitalist societies and the Soviet Union was not so important for both sides. The Stalinist bureaucracy's perverted use of the Marxist ideology has created an immense problem for those radicals who wanted to promote an alternative to liberalism and conservatism. But the fact that Karl Marx still interests so many could be explained by the still important need to search for alternatives but also as a reflection of the power of his ideas.

Marxism has had strong critics among liberals, conservatives and others since its development in the nineteenth century but after the failure of the European working-class movement in the early 1920s, it was increasingly questioned, changed and attacked by Marxist radicals and other left-wing intellectuals, especially by those who preferred reforms and order to revolutions and disorder. After the Second World War, the attacks coming from within the radical left camp increased in their hope to find justification for their own failure. The post-war boom with successful capitalist economies, growth, higher living standards for ordinary people and social democracy with promotion of the welfare state created even more problems for dogmatic Stalinism and Western Marxism because capitalism did not behave in the way they had been claiming it would. Capitalism did not collapse on its own as predicted by some of them but, on the contrary, led to better conditions of life for ordinary people. Many finished by concluding that there were actually no limits to growth in capitalist societies. They had finally turned away from analyzing the material conditions and limitations of the system to more romantic, cultural and psychological critiques of society.

Marxism became only a sociological, intellectual and academic subject with no longer any relation with politics and political conflicts. The materialist and economic framework of society was ignored and only the superficial appearances created by society were discussed. Ideas such as the dictatorship of the proletariat and the importance of the working class as agents of social change were replaced by ideas that ordinary people were to blame for the horrors of World War Two, that they were easily led by the power of advertising, media and now internet. It is useful to note here that the contempt for ordinary people and for their quality as rational agents was already present. Ordinary people were seen as easily-manipulated people. Radical theories and critiques moved from production in society to consumption in society. From the working class defined by their social position in production i.e. as workers, radicals concentrated upon individuals as consumers, developing analyses of different modes of consumption. From the productive working class as political agents, radicals moved to the idea that their role as consumers would be the place to look for political agency. When we consider identity politics, we can see that this notion has been completely accepted. All identities are social identities in consumer society. The important social relations of production are discounted as if a society can exist only on consumption or as if the particular social relations, related to how a particular society is organized around production, are simply natural and eternal.

Marxist intellectuals such as those from the Institute for Social Research at Frankfurt rejected historical materialism all together and turned further into psychological analysis, cultural and linguistic explanations. Horkheimer, as the new director in 1930, changed the research areas away from historical materialism as a "science," toward a development of "social philosophy" supplemented by empirical investigations.[53] Marcuse, another member of the Frankfurt School, argued in 1964, in his *One-Dimensional Man*, that contemporary Western society creates "artificially" needs and interests and manipulates the working class through consumerism and the mass media. Thus it was irrational to consider them as potential agents of social change as Karl Marx had argued.[54]

The New Left movement, in the West, was not homogenous and was influenced by a wide range of ideas. It developed out of the disillusion with Stalinism, but also from the left's political defeat in convincing the working class with their ideas and mostly arose out of the student radicalism of the 1960s. The American New Left was influenced by the civil rights movement and the Frankfurt School which saw students and academics as the agents of social change, and rejected Soviet communism, orthodox Marxism and social democracy. The main organization was the Students for a Democratic Society with Tom Hayden as its founder and first president. With the Port Huron statement, a political manifesto published in 1962, they called for a new movement which "must give form to the feelings of helplessness and indifference, so that people may see the political, social, and economic sources of their private troubles and organize society." The university was seen as playing an essential role because it "is located in a permanent position of social influence" and is "the central institution for organizing, evaluating, and transmitting knowledge." Students and academics in universities, essentially individuals from the middle class, were called to form this new movement showing their belief that students and academics rather than the working class were the important agents for social transformation.[55] In the 1960s, the end of the post-war boom led to a revival of class conflicts but also to an increase in the radicalization of the middle class as seen with the New Left. Their politics, based on middle-class interests, took over any other radical politics originally based on classical Marxist politics and working-class interests.

The British New Left developed in the late 1950s and was also influenced by Italian political theorist Antonio Gramsci, the Frankfurt School with Herbert Marcuse, American sociologist C. Wright Mills and structuralist and post-structuralist thinkers such as Louis Althusser and Michel Foucault. British theorists such as Stuart Hall, Raymond Williams and Richard Hoggart were some of the first developing the new analysis and ideas about culture and mass media, especially after the formation of the Centre for Cultural Studies in Birmingham. Culture was no longer seen as reflecting the forces and social relations of production. It became important in and of itself. There is nothing wrong in trying to understand cultural phenomenon but the focus on them at a time when other social and economic phenomena are seen as natural and permanent encourages the belief that only appearances need to be changed. Is it so surprising that this focus on mass media, advertising, culture and psychology led to a gradual acceptance of the now common view of people as simply manipulated and weak individuals? The radicals' turn to education as a tool for cultural and social change is imitating the liberal view of the world. Radicals have moved from supporting ordinary people and seeing their historical potential to blaming them for defeats, blaming their psychology for easy political indoctrination at school and university. It is no longer difficult, for them, to blame the white working class, some of the less powerful people in society, for racism, discrimination and oppression apparently suffered by black middle and upper classes, some of the most powerful people in society. The political, social and economic power exercised by the working class from all backgrounds is nothing comparable to the power exercised by the middle class and is even more insignificant when compared with the power upper class and ruling elites possess. And yet, when discussing racism and anti-racism, we are meant to forget about this and divide the world between white oppressors and oppressed blacks.

This interpretation of the world is a major obstacle for a productive fight against racism. If my white neighbor does not like my skin color, it is his problem as long as it does not prevent me from enjoying my house, accessing health services or getting a job. But I know his life, social and economic interests are much more similar to mine than Beyonce's life and interests will ever be. Building solidarity with him in order to change the world so that most of us can have access to proper health services, education, good working conditions, good wages or a clean environment is more productive than building solidarity, simply because of our similar skin color, with other black people who may actually want to keep the world as it is, with a majority of people not accessing the wealth and knowledge humanity is producing.

James Heartfield, in his book The "Death of the Subject" explained, provided an interesting account of how the autonomous Subject, the rational, independent and active person, has been degraded by Western intellectuals. The symptoms, such as infantilization with "confusions around the adult-child distinction," emasculation when "masculine" traits are seen as problems and a common view of ourselves and society in pathological terms are well established today.[56] The view of the inner self as vulnerable and isolated and the promotion of identities, where the level of

149

oppression and suffering is used as a factor to determine the quality and position of the importance of identities, both reflect and are the consequences of this attitude over the Subject. A victim mentality is developed and supported because it has become common to look at the victims who have suffered the most as those who should have louder voices, more resources and more authority. The more they can prove their suffering and victim status, the worthier they are for others to support as a valid cause. Radicals, counter-culture, left and liberals who embraced identity politics for themselves, imitating the ideas of the ruling elites and the racists promoting racial thinking, have given up on the idea of a strong and rational humanity with a potential to transform itself and the world. As I wrote before, the Enlightenment ideals had been rejected by most traditions long before the twentieth century but what we witness today is the last bastion, those who saw themselves as the radical left, also rejecting all humanist and Enlightenment ideals as well as Marx's thoughts on society, progress, human emancipation, individual full development, freedom and possibilities for social change. These rejections also explain why radical activists are, today, more concerned with moralizing than developing political ideas. But changing the world rationally and collectively starts with the political agents. Let's see a few more of the ideas that have been abandoned by the left-wing camp which now support identity-based anti-racism.

First, Karl Marx did not develop his understanding of the capitalist social organization simply because of his moral opposition to exploitation. Exploitation existed in previous societies. Extremely harsh conditions of living for most of the world's population were not unique to developing capitalism. He believed that it was possible to rationally and scientifically understand a specific human society, its unique "mode of production" and "historical form of social process of production." Criticizing what he called "vulgar economy" which only looked at the "outward appearances of economic relations" and endorsed the concepts developed by those defending the status quo, he rightly reminded us that "all science would be superfluous if the outward appearance and the essence of things directly coincided."[57] His theories on the capitalist society led him to understand what he thought were the positive aspects and limitations of this particular society. He combined the abstract notion of universalism of the Enlightenment with a particularism based on the specific material basis of the capitalist society. With his development of historical materialism, he united universalism with particularism, the abstract with the concrete. He understood the historically specific social relations of production as the place where the particular should be found. Today, unfortunately, the concrete is seen in the world of our cultural and interpersonal relationships such as racial or national relationships and other currently promoted social identities.

Marx was a humanist who was interested in human emancipation and in the full development of the individual in society. He understood that for humans to be free, they had to overcome material constraints, such as food production, which limit human beings' ability to make decisions and choices. To overcome the material constraints dominating humanity, the development of the productive forces of society is essential. He rejected the abstract concept of freedom promoted by liberalism. Freedom cannot simply be an act of will and he argued:

> It is possible to achieve real liberation only in the real world and by real means...Slavery cannot be abolished without the steam engine and the mule jenny, serfdom cannot be abolished without improved agriculture, and...in general, people cannot be liberated as long as they are unable to obtain food and drink, housing and clothing in adequate quality and quantity.[58]

It is clear that the possibility of an individual to express fully his individuality within society depends on his ability to decide free from material constraints and from domination by others. His concept of freedom here seems more related to the Republican concept – freedom as non-domination – we discussed earlier than the liberal concept of freedom as non-interference. But the historically specific nature of his notion of freedom is quite distinct. Discussing the important question of alienation, Mészáros explained Marx's concept of freedom as being in three parts which are linked to each other. The first part is the degree of "freedom from natural necessity" which depends on the productivity of labor and the specific stage of human development. Social progress allows us to move further away from nature's domination. "Freedom from the interfering power of other men" is, in a way, a little similar to the Republican concept of freedom as non-domination. A specific level of freedom from natural necessity could be reached but it does not necessarily mean the majority of humanity will enjoy the result of this. This depends on the kind of social relations of production existing in a particular society. The third aspect is the "freedom to more fully exercise Man's essential powers," the powers that distinguish human beings from the rest of nature. Labor or human activity as "free activity" is one essential power. It is not determined by necessity and mere survival and thus does not include activity related to our animal functions such as eating or procreating. The "power of Man to objectify himself through his labour" is another essential power. Humans can put something of themselves in the work they do and thus can "see" themselves in what they have created. Sociality is a third essential power. It is also a very important characteristic of humanity, making human beings "universal" beings.[59] Our sociality is at the root of all aspects of our lives; progress, knowledge, society or science are dependent on this human trait.

Clearly, the Republican or Marx's concepts of freedom are

concepts no longer widely discussed today unfortunately. Maybe because, with his analysis, Marx had argued that capitalism did not make humanity freer in all these different aspects. Nonetheless, we can analyze the advance humanity has made so far when discussing freedom and capitalism; the importance of real human needs which are historically specific, the higher productivity of labor or the idea of equality simply as abstract equality of right-bearing individuals are important questions in this discussion.

We can see how far the idea of freedom has changed today when the contemporary notion of individual development and individual freedom is the demand we turn inwards in our own mind, to develop or discover our individual identity. One of the underlying assumptions that make this notion readily accepted is to believe we already live in a world where most rights-bearing individuals are free in liberal democracies. Another common assumption is to believe that the conditions of our lives are natural and permanent, that there is no alternative except trying to get the best out of our current situation. Thus, the conclusion is to think that the only barriers to liberal freedom are a lack of knowledge of oneself and/or, in the case of black liberation, obstructions from society's institutions, laws and norms. Christopher Lebron argued that "a refreshed radical black politics" had to face "basic failure of imagination, fear of what directly confronting power requires of each of us, or simple lack of motivation." And yet what he suggested was to use "shameful publicity" to let others know that the "idea and ideal of American democracy" is great but that in practice, "very few of the benefits available to whites are freely or fairly available to blacks." "Shameful publicity sets the terms of moral and ethical acknowledgment on those acceptable to complainants," he declared. Another suggestion for his "radical ethics" is to "countercolonize the white imagination" with black people, struggling against social inequality, rewriting the images white people have of black people. Demand for whites to acknowledge that "blacks are worthy of a respect that whites take for granted" is another part of his radical ethics while acting with "unfragmented compassion" and to be "prepared to enter into relationships defined by reciprocity and mutual regard" with "white humanity" is also suggested as part of the "refreshed radical black politics."[60] It is not difficult to see that his world is simply divided into races with one racial group oppressing the other. After accepting this division where one race is blamed for the social inequality, he is mostly appealing to the group he sees as oppressor to help redress the situation of the vulnerable black Americans. There are no discussions about the material and economic circumstances that led to racial inequalities. Apparently, only the wrong attitude from white people and policies are considered in his "radical black politics." To push his points, past thinkers are used as if there is a straightforward continuity between them and those who are currently supporting the Black Lives Matter movement, giving us the impression that nothing has changed since the lives of Ida B. Wells and Frederick Douglass.

Development of liberal-left identity politics

When considering the issue of race, culture and nation, it becomes clear that identity politics did not start in the second half of the twentieth century with the help of the radicals and liberals mentioned above but in the nineteenth century by those using race, culture and national character to define their identities. These past identities were based on the old meaning of identity but they were still social identities. They specifically put people into distinct and discreet categories and were seen as causally determining individuals' moral and mental characteristics. These social identities were politicized to be the basis of interests, political positions and political debates. Today, Gay groups use identity politics to fight for their specific interests against society seen as the enemy. In the past, white identity proponents or racists used identity politics to fight for their specific racial interests defined by the belief that the white race had distinct interests. As we have seen in the chapter discussing race as a product of history, Ivan Hannaford had looked at the historical relationship between politics, religion and race and had shown that "principles of civil association" were "in opposition to race in Western civilization."[61] If we understand politics as with notions of the polis and polity, then we can see that politicized social identities are anti-political. The polis is understood as an association of equals but identities based on social and racial inequalities are not equal.

There are, of course, differences between identity politics of the past and present. Today, identities are based on the contemporary view of the individual as vulnerable, weak, sick and in need of protection. The degradation of the Subject, the further atomization of society, the search for psychological solutions to social problems, the therapeutic culture and the culture of fear led to a view of the self and individual as weak, subject to medical conditions, isolated and threatened by all around. Sociologist Frank Furedi stated that the current cultural phenomenon leads more to the "promotion of self-limitation" and the "distancing of the self from others" than to the "realisation of self-fulfilment." "It posits the self in distinctly fragile and feeble form" with an increasing need of experts to manage life. Thus, it "both reflects and promotes the trend towards fragmentation and alienation."[62] While I disagree with the idea that identity politics is a new phenomenon only developed in the mid-twentieth century, I agree that the contemporary form of identity politics is the "first movement to internalize the therapeutic ideal" and that through "identity politics the preoccupations of the self are converted into a wider group identity."[63] The form that identity politics took was influenced by the current therapeutic culture becoming increasingly influential in the second half of the twentieth century. Historian Elisabeth Lasch-Quinn, in her book *Race Experts: How Racial Etiquette, Sensitivity, Training, and New Age Therapy Hijacked the Civil Rights Revolution,* argued that the increasing preoccupation with the place of white activists in the black power movement, for example, was due to an increased concern in asserting a black identity defined progressively in therapeutic terms. Sociologist Philip Rieff had argued that a cultural shift in modern society had replaced "religion as the dominant way of understanding the world" with psychotherapy and thus individualism and obsession with the inner self becoming the main focus.[64] Therefore, modern identity politics is also the product of the abandonment by radicals of universalist and humanist politics. Radicals embraced the idea of cultures and of politics stressing differences between cultural, racial and social groups, arguing that to fight social injustice, defending each distinct group separately is more effective than universalist Marxist politics. And this was a tragedy when universalism was finally abandoned by radicals in order for them to imitate divisive political ideas developed by those who benefited from racial thinking in the first place.

Class politics, in its original sense, was not identity politics but the political form that the aim for *universal human emancipation* took after understanding the basis of capitalist society. The early aim of Marxism was political action for human freedom. István Mészáros recalled Marx's view:

> Thus although the fundamental governing principle of the new society is *economic* (as opposed to the essentially *political* regulative principle of feudal society), it cannot be divorced from the political framework in which it operates. Therefore the task of "universal human emancipation" must be formulated "in the *political form* of the emancipation of the workers."[65]

The classes were not defined as identities. Class politics were based on an understanding of workers as the rational agents of social change, not based on the romantic, emotional, faith-based or identitarian definitions used to explain the support for workers today. It was a politics of freedom, based on the belief that workers needed to overcome social obstacles in order to create a classless and freer society. Although Hannah Arendt misunderstood Marxism as politics based on economic determinism, she thought the classical meaning of politics associated politics with freedom. She argued that the aim of political action and the reason for the development of politics was freedom. It was only in our modern age that the aim of politics had become security and life interests. Politics was originally concerned with the world and not with life itself.[66] With such an understanding of politics, we can see not only that identity politics is not politics but also most of our political world is not concerned with freedom and political issues but with social, economic and private issues.

Working-class politics can only be interpreted as identity politics when "working class" is seen as an identity defined by a particular culture, way of life and ways of thinking rather than understood as an economic and social class. The support for the working class can become more of a support or a preference for a specific identity, a faith in them rather than a particular understanding of the world which put the working class at the center of universalist politics. Still, the question radical politics has to answer is whether seeing the working class as the universal class is still the right idea for the twenty-first century capitalist system.

The notions of race, culture and identity politics which developed against Enlightenment ideals are seen as progressive by most political sides today. The only difference is in the cultures and identities supported by various sides. Those claiming to oppose left-liberal identity politics and the promotion of particular cultures are often happy to promote cultures and identities they think acceptable such as the "native culture," "western culture," "working-class identity" or political positions which are now only seen through identity politics such as the "liberal identity," "democrat identity," "Brexiter identity" or "Remainer identity." Two researchers analyzing online comments found that "Brexiters used certain terms, or categories, to 'define' the attributes of someone who belonged to the Remainer camp, and vice versa." Those definitions were labels such as "scaremonger" or "racist." Once these political positions are seen and acted upon as if they were identities, the solutions proposed to stop the disputes are also non-political such as feeling British as a "larger identity." Thus, the researchers argued that *"social psychologically* informed measures could be used to try and *heal social* divisions"[67] (italics are mine). Developing political arguments to convince members of the opposite political side is not considered a solution because this is no longer a political dispute but a competition between identities. If social and political problems are only understood in terms of culture and identity and if politics is only seen through identity politics, anti-racist activists need to ask if it is so surprising to see an increase in the support for white identity?

Identity politics, defined as the use of politicized social identities in politics, developed in the nineteenth century but the expression "identity politics" is thought to have been first read in April 1977. It was found in the political statement of a black feminist group, based in Boston, called the Combahee River Collective (CRC). The group was originally part of the National Black Feminist Organisation (NBFO), founded in 1973 in New York. Even though "identity politics" was not used as an expression, we know that identity and the politics of identity was already an important concern among social movements activists calling for the liberation of blacks, women and gays. The NBFO original statement in 1973 claimed that *"We,* not white men or black men, must define our own self-image" and that they had to "continue to remind the black liberation Movement that there can't be liberation for half the race" showing their frustration with the movement they had been supporting.[68]

Barbara Smith, Beverly Smith and Demita Frazier, with their CRC statement, expressed well a particular step in black feminism history. They still believed in the possibility of radical social transformation with a universalist basis for their politics of liberation. They were still committed to fighting for a new world where all oppressions (racial, gender, sexuality, class and imperialism) had disappeared. However, they also show a concern in developing a new politics of subjectivity which would include a positive identity for black women. To build better radical political ideas for their own situation as black women dealing with racism, sexism and working-class issues, they thought they had to base them from their own personal experiences, their own identity rather than others' experiences.[69] This belief that their personal experiences can be the basis for political analysis, theories and intellectual development came from their "experience and disillusionment" built up after their involvement with black liberation movements (civil rights, black nationalism and the Black Panthers) and the traditional left-wing political groups. Their feelings of abandonment were certainly based on reality. The position of women in black liberation movements was not considered important or appropriate to worry about by many activists. The traditional left concerns were often focused on the exploitation of workers while racism and sexism were ignored or even supported. Furthermore, the feminist movement was mainly concerned with white middle-class women's problems and experiences. The political isolation of these groups and the failure of the labor movement and left-wing political groups to develop universalist radical politics have led to a progressive turn toward political ideas highlighting differences of culture, experiences, subjectivity and identity.

The understanding of human beings as beings with specific cultural identities and the construction of racism as a psychological and behavioral problem had an enormous effect on the anti-racism movement. Overt expressions of racism were increasingly seen as immoral, as unsophisticated or as the acts of an uneducated person. Ideas that seem right-wing or conservative were marginalized after the war, because of the experiences of Nazism and fascism. But racial thinking was not opposed but reworked. Racial divisions are still accepted as permanent, a product of human psychology, social experiences or biology. Leah N Gordon, in her book *From Power to Prejudice: The Rise of Racial Individualism in Midcentury America*, analyzed the development of what she calls "racial individualism" in academia and among the intellectual activists involved in the issue of race and racism in the United States. Racial individualism developed between the end of the Second World War and the early 1960s and became the dominant framework used to understand the issue of race and racism; the preference for it is due to its often hard-to-see conservative potential. The post-war boom and the shift in American liberalism which became less critical of the economic order, the Cold War, anti-communism and the rejection of radical left-wing politics that used to suggest structural and economic interpretations of racism, the extensive influence of psychology are aspects of the context in which racial individualism became so influential. Gordon argued that:

> Bringing together psychological individualism, rights-based individualism, and belief in the socially transformative power of education, racial individualism presented prejudice and discrimination as the root cause of racial conflict, focused on individuals in the study of race relations, and suggested that racial justice could be attained by changing white minds and protecting African American rights.[70]

We have seen that changing individuals' minds and education was also the solution proposed by UNESCO. The numerous types of training such as racial bias training, racial and cultural awareness training, racial diversity workshops, offered in workplaces, universities, schools and other institutions, are examples showing the popularity of racial individualism.

Elisabeth Lasch-Quinn has shown how social engineers and experts took over the American civil rights movement targeting people's minds and prejudices with their new enterprises such as "racial identity theory," "oppression pedagogy," "diversity training," "interracial etiquette," "ethnotherapy," "cultural reeducation." Lasch-Quinn rightly argued that these activists and intellectuals moved away from the earlier universalism of the civil rights movement.[71] "I am a man" was reflecting the past demand for equal treatment, for equal rights. Today, "I am a black man" promotes the idea that the race defines the man and that difference in race should be accepted and respected. The particular has taken over the universal. But more importantly, she argued that this was not a simple move from a focus on citizen rights to the "black voice." This was not inevitable. As she noted:

The idea that there exists a single, unified black consciousness, beyond a shared sense that wrongs had been inflicted upon blacks in the American past, was a product of the radical milieu as it unfolded in the cultural context of the age. That race was a pre-eminently psychological matter had become so widely believed by the 1960s that the notion of an individual's coming into racial awareness – or a society's rising consciousness of race – was reduced to narrow models for blacks and whites. For blacks, this consciousness involved freedom from psychological and emotional repression, mainly self-affirmation through the release of rage or another form of self-assertion. For whites, it meant freedom from the alleged psychological debilitation of their own racism.[72]

"White guilt" has become the way in which some white people, especially white liberals, have expressed themselves in order to show their awareness of racism and their own racism. Being aware of the life experiences of black people has become a way of attenuating their feelings of guilt. Whether they have agreed with racist ideas or not, the claim that their white race makes them racist is promoted. The original sin, in the white population, apparently forces individuals to act on it in order to purify their moral being and their soul. There is no fight to transcend racial divisions, to act on the world. Social transformations that would change our lives and the world around us have been replaced by therapeutic means to help passive and emotional human beings who have to live with and suffer in an out-of-their-control world. But the consequences of these changes are bad for all. Social critic Shelby Steele explained well the current attraction for claims of racism and the constant racialization of every single issue today:

> The most striking irony of the age of white guilt is that racism suddenly became *valuable* to the people who had suffered it. Racism, in the age of racism, had only brought every variety of inhuman treatment, which is why the King generation felt that extinguishing it would bring equality. But in the age of white guilt, racism was also *evidence* of white wrongdoing and, therefore, evidence of white obligation to blacks. King had argued that whites were obligated to morality and democratic principles. But white guilt meant they were obligated to black *people* because they needed the moral authority only black people could bestow.[73]

White guilt has become a valuable currency for some black individuals but the opposition to racial divisions has been abandoned by the mainstream anti-racist movement. But how deep is this white guilt when individuals are not responsible for the past actions and the social problems of today? Feeling guilty about our own actions has real meaning and can involve deep emotions because it involves our conscience and moral responsibility. But when decisions and actions were made by others, all there is is a superficial feeling important only in a society where appearances, superficiality and conformism are seen as qualities.

Trump's election, Brexit, the French Gilets Jaunes protesting for more than a year, the French general strikes over Macron's retirement reform, Hong Kong demonstrations for more democracy, the civil protests in Lebanon, the Haitian protests, the worldwide migrants issue and many other events across the world have made class conflicts visible. And yet, many of the Western radicals and left-wing groups are focused on identity politics and are moralizing about the terrible life conditions rather than building a real radical and political alternative to oppose the foundations that created these terrible conditions in the first place. Worse, by concentrating on identity politics, they have become willing participants in the ruling elites' clampdown on ordinary people. Bayard Rustin understood very well the danger in ignoring the class issue when discussing racial discrimination. As he noted, if a black worker sees the problem he faces only through the prism of race, "he will inevitably find himself the ally of the white capitalist against the white worker" and will become a pawn used by management against other workers. All workers will lose. If, while still recognizing the issue of racism, he acknowledges the problem of poverty, "he will be aligned with the white worker against management."[74] This solidarity with other workers will help them fight together to demand better wages, better working conditions, better work benefits, better housing, better education. This is also true for any other group of people. The promotion of identity politics today leads to a destruction of solidarity between workers. We are supposed to highlight differences between "black workers," "white workers," "female workers," "male workers," "Muslim workers," "Christian workers," "Gay workers," "Transsexual workers" and accept that all of them have different interests at work. Identity politics is a very useful tool to fragment ordinary people into small identity groups, siding with employers and management in order to challenge other workers. Recognizing common interests within the working class does not mean ignoring the consequences of racial inequalities. It means recognizing the political ideas that would help us fight exploitation, oppression and discrimination to eventually achieve human emancipation.

The book *From #BlackLivesMatter to Black Liberation* written by Keeanga-Yamahtta Taylor, who is part of the American left, is interesting in regard to this tension between identity politics and class politics. Although the premise of her book is still that black people are the most oppressed and that their main barrier to a better life is racism, one can feel the constant tension between this claim and the realization that ordinary people from all backgrounds are actually attacked by the American police and by the state. With all the material she collected, she still refused to address the point that her research leads to: police violence, the militarization of the police, the constant attacks by the justice system and the degradation of services are affecting the whole lower-class population across all backgrounds and this is not mainly a racism issue. The solidarity between people because they belong to a similar race is given priority over solidarity built between people because of their common social and political interests and goals. Racial groupings are seen as superior to collective actions by people who have been convinced they have similar political interests and goals. By moving from universalist class politics to identity politics, radicals have stopped being political. Only a moral left exists today when there is an urgent need for a political left.

Importance of politics

Christopher Kyriakides and Rodolfo Torres proposed that human beings as "hopeful subjects," as future-oriented agents, are negated when they are seen through the prism of race. Identifying the contemporary widespread sense of limits and of pessimism vis-à-vis humanity's potentials, the authors argued that we need hope again and a new politics of possibility. Hope, here, is not simply a psychological and personal attitude but is also based on recognizing the importance of reason, the transformative aspect of human actions on the world, and the open-ended future due to humanity's creative and active abilities.[75] In the classical understanding of politics we have discussed previously, hope is the foundation for the existence of the political world. Much of the contemporary political debates are about discussing technical and managerial solutions in order to administer and control the current social order. With no hope and visions for the future, the concerns are about the technicality of sharing resources perceived as limited and about balancing what are seen as the different interests of competing groups in order to keep and save a certain order.

Wolin observed that there has been a decline in political thought since the beginning of the nineteenth century through "the erosion of the distinctively political" although John Rawls revived political philosophy in the second half of the twentieth century. The decline started with the introduction of the sociological notion of "society," common to Lockean liberalism but also to conservatism, socialism, anarchism and managerialism.[76] We see the decline with identity politics today when we have replaced the political category "citizen" with the social categories "man," "women," "white" and "black."

Politics developed because of the ability of rational and social human beings to act collectively in order to create the world they want. "One cannot speak about politics without also speaking about freedom; and one cannot speak about freedom without also speaking about politics,"[77] claimed Hannah Arendt. It is through politics and political actions in the world that human beings struggle to create a new world where they can be free. She argued that fighting to get the necessities of life like in primitive societies is not a political action. If our concerns are only about sharing resources and preserving lives, why should we be worried about living under democracy, oligarchy or dictatorship? A healthy political world is essential for human social development. The rational and political world is the common world we can all enter to communicate together. The observation that many in the younger generations are not worried about a lack of freedom and more concerned about security and safety reflects the appalling state of our political and public world.

The development of a political realm was a very important step in human history. As I said before, political thought originated with the ancient Greeks and it developed when the Greeks stopped seeing humanity and society as part of nature and as simply following the same laws of nature. The notion that nature could be understood with human reason was an important step in human development. Classical politics distinguishes between the political order and the natural order. The political order is a man-made world but more importantly a common order created to deal with the concerns shared by all members of the political community.[78] The "nature of a good life for an individual" will not necessarily be defined the same way as the "nature of a good life for the community." In fact, the understanding of society and what it means to be an individual and the question concerning the relationship between the two have been important concerns since the ancient Greeks. For example, the understanding of society differs between various political ideologies and schools of thought. "For the conservative, society is naturally hierarchical" and humans "are not born free and equal, rational and independent" but with a "complex web" of "custom and tradition, which provide them with security and discipline and give meaning to their lives." For the pluralist thinkers, society is a "harmonious network of groups, organizations and associations, which both influence and compete for the loyalties of individuals." Liberalism, with its "political individualism," sees "independent and rational beings, who are the sole generators of their own wants" and "the best judges of their own interests." Thus, in early liberalism, society was understood as established through a social contract between individuals. Today, participation in free elections is portrayed as the consent between individuals.[79] Marxists understand human beings as social beings who create their individuality and find meanings only through the other social beings. If we understand human beings as social beings, then we can also see that the political ideal of individual freedom is an historical phenomenon which could only be conceived after a decrease in the domination of nature over society. The capitalist development, its rise in labor productivity and collaborative productive activity provided a better space for its further development. But we can see the importance of politics both for the individuals trying to achieve their individual potential and for the society where social beings live.

The members in the political realm are the citizens who are prepared to take responsibility for the community or the world. In ancient Greece, the relationship between individuals and community was much more balanced than it is today because of the stronger domination of nature over society as a whole. The citizens are not defined by their natural attributes but by their commitment to being involved in participating in decisions and actions with the aim of creating a good life for the community. These actions, for the Greeks and Romans, included defending the community and dispensing justice. Currently, "citizens" are defined by attributes such as races, cultures, identities or birthplace. These are not political characteristics but social and personal characteristics which are being politicized. But by politicizing these social characteristics, the important political world is damaged, and society stays depoliticized. Politics is not denying the particular interests of different sections of society. In the political world, human beings recognize the different interests and conflicts in the community and apply together human reason to resolve these conflicts with the purpose of improving the common good. But the common good was not defined by the necessities of life. These were part of the household activities, the private realm. And of course, resolving political conflicts will, inevitably, create new ones. Thus, politics is a constant relationship between resolving conflicts and creating new conflicts.[80]

Going nowhere with anti-racist ideas based on identity

Critical race theory is based on the argument that "races are categories that society invents, manipulates, or retires when convenient."[81] We have seen in the first chapter that this is the wrong way to understand the race issue. Race is a social category but more importantly it is a product of human history. Racial thinking, which developed the concept and category of race, arose at a particular historical moment and through the conflicts of new and old social groups in the developing capitalist society. The capitalist society which mainly grew out of the feudal society destroyed old relations of production and old social groups such as serfdom, peasants, aristocracy. The capitalist class and working class and the new capitalist system developed through conflicts between all these old and new social groups. With humanity's understanding of itself, nature and society, social inequalities were interpreted as racial inequalities. The concept of race is not fixed so we do need to understand what this concept means in the twentieth-first century. Racialization of groups of people carries on, for example, but the divisions and the consequences of these divisions in our contemporary globalized world are not the same as in the past. In the Western world, people are often seen as irrational, gullible and vulnerable beings. The explanations for our world will not be the same as when humanity believed in itself and its ability to control its destiny.

Critical race theory and intersectionality reflect this retreat from political thought and political vision. The notion that "everyone has potentially conflicting, overlapping identities, loyalties, and allegiances" is certainly not an original idea.[82] What is interesting is to note that this notion is thought a useful idea in politics. In the political realm where citizens discuss social issues in order to create a common world accepted by all, it is not the fact that citizens represent individuals with diverse lives, histories, personalities and social identities that is important and productive but the notion that to create a common and just society where all can live together, diverse interests coming from various social groups have to be recognized and discussed and compromises made. Politics is not about what an individual with his limitless collection of identities can get for his own personal life but how different social groups can create a common vision for the society they want at a particular time. The turn into focusing on our social and personal identities, even though these identities will be often politicized, i.e. used in "political" discussions, is anti-political, does not attack social barriers some groups have to deal with and does not resolve our current social issues.

The view that politics of identities is anti-political needs to be emphasized here because it really shows how it offers no prospects for progress to anybody interested in creating a better world for most of us. The notions of the common good and human liberation have nearly disappeared in contemporary Western society where each identity group fights for its own interests regardless of the consequences for the future of humanity or society as a whole. These identity groups are getting smaller and smaller, more fragmented to allow for more particular and personal demands. These fragmented identities reflect the atomized society where individuals are portrayed as isolated, vulnerable and threatened by all others. A recent identity group, discussed in the United States, is the American Descendants of Slavery or ADOS. It seems to be more of an online phenomenon for now, but this identity group argues that black Americans need a separate ethnic identity to differentiate themselves from Caribbean and African blacks who immigrated later.[83] This identity group is based on the tensions and hostility between black Americans and new black immigrants and it is based on the belief that black immigrants who came voluntarily to the United States are taking benefits that should be for black Americans whose ancestors were brought in chains and had to suffer from slavery.

The politics of identity is dividing the population into small groups viciously fighting each other to defend their own specific interests. Solidarity through recognizing common political and social interests and the important knowledge that collective actions are essential in a fight for better lives have greatly diminished since the abandonment of universalist politics by radical and social movements.

This new form of identity politics reflects the contemporary preoccupation with the self and thus to question someone's identity or personhood is seen as the worse transgression. To question or attack the claims of an identity group is understood as a personal attack, as questioning the inner self of members of the group. Each of these groups are becoming more individualized in the search for their inner self. But this focus on individual personal experiences leads to an increasing lack of empathy for others. The therapeutic culture, as we saw earlier, both reflects and promotes the atomization of society as well as the sense of alienation individuals feel today. Identities internalize this and thus the competition between identities is progressively becoming a cruel competition between atomized, isolated and vulnerable individuals. Virtue is decided not on the quality of individuals' actions and decisions but on their suffering. To claim an understanding of victimhood in general and to declare one's own suffering has become the manner in which one is considered worthy of sympathy. But in the hierarchy of suffering, individuals have to ignore others' suffering to promote themselves. They are creating a world which denies the possibility for empathy, compassion and solidarity with others who do not belong to the group.

In an article entitled "How Did the Holocaust Supersede American Genocide and Slavery?",[84] the author is wondering why Americans focus on the "Jewish Holocaust" as she called it, when America has its own racist atrocities and "Holocausts." To argue for a better place in the current oppression Olympics, she claimed that the focus on the Holocaust is due to the fact that Jews were not "darker-skinned people." Apparently, "fair-skinned people" sufferings are more easily remembered than "darker-skinned people" because "White and White passing Americans" are "erasing parts of American history." She then proceeds to tell us how the atrocities she claimed to be concerned about are "worse" and so, rather than the Holocaust, they should be the focus for Americans. The support for *racial thinking* and *eugenics* ideas which led to the *systematic extermination* of groups of people in our very recent past should not be the focus in America because, in a previous period full of cruelty and hardship, a greater number of people were enslaved, badly treated and killed. Understanding the significance of events is now done through discussing numbers of deaths and through preferred identities.

Only specific oppressed groups can speak of certain issues because they are seen as personal experiences owned by the members of the group. No questions or criticism of these issues are possible even though the groups are still asking for sympathy. How is sympathy possible in these circumstances, especially with a competition in suffering? But identity politics is not a religion, a cult or a contagious loss of mind. It is a continuation of what politics has been in our modern era but, with the recent added approval by those who used to promote universalist ideas within the damaging influences of our contemporary therapeutic culture. The argument I am making is that the reduction of people to a race, culture, sexuality, nationality, religion, lifestyle, education, medical condition in order to create new identities, to politicize these identities and to fight for particular interests has damaged our political realm for too long now. This rejection of politics has taken different forms, depending on the social, economic and intellectual circumstances. But Western societies have moved away from politics since the reactions against the Enlightenment and democratic radicalism. It is time for those concerned with freedom and with the creation of a better world to develop new universalist politics with new visions of the future. It was done before and it can be done again.

Conclusion

The contemporary anti-racism movement based on identity politics is counterproductive, anti-political, keeps the status quo with racial thinking, helps those in power with their need to keep their position in society, divides society along racial, cultural and identitarian lines and raises barriers between those who need to be political allies. The current ideas of this movement are built on counter-Enlightenment, anti-radical tradition and anti-humanist visions of human beings and society; they need to be opposed if we want to transcend social and racial divisions.

Trusting others and taking them seriously as potential allies

Today, we are constantly told we are not rational but emotional, selfish, destructive and hateful creatures set on destroying each other and the environment around us. If this were true, what would be the point of considering anti-racism? If someone has such a strong dislike of humanity, would it not be reasonable to conclude that their anti-racism position is simply a tool to claim moral superiority over others? I am not an expert, nor do I have all the answers. I am one of the privileged people who can have access to at least part of humanity's knowledge. My parents did not have this opportunity and many today still do not have it as a consequence of social and economic inequalities. These inequalities disturb me greatly and make me angry but I have hope. I also strongly believe that we, rational human beings, can understand the world and can collectively transform it. Faith, hope, utopia, drive? We can call this what we want but this hope is what helped us create a world where most of us do not spend most of our time foraging for food and water. Thus, I hope to oppose racial thinking, the racialization of *all* people and the resulting racial divisions. The racialization of *any* group is wrong including the racialization of immigrants today. I am not supporting one racial, cultural or identitarian group over another. As civil rights activist Bayard Rustin said decades ago: "(O)ne has to fight for justice for all. If I do not fight bigotry wherever it is, bigotry is thereby strengthened. And to the degree that it is strengthened, it will thereby have the power to turn on me."[1] Bayard Rustin had recognized the importance of politics and of endorsing the potential universal character of struggles for equal rights and equal opportunity. There are people who simply hate and want to dominate and exploit other human beings. But many others, in this world, are hoping for a world where their race, culture or identity are not used as weapons against them to dominate them, discriminate against them, exploit them or even kill them. Therefore, we need to ask whether we are in a period of human history where the potential for such a world already exists and if so, what are the obstacles we need to overcome or destroy before this potential can be realized.

To answer these questions, "we must create conditions where disagreement can take place without fear of exclusion and excommunication."[2] The abuse and condemnation Mark Fisher was describing must stop if we really want to develop ideas and solutions. It does not mean we must agree with each other or stop judging and criticizing ideas. On the contrary, the personal attacks must stop so that we can concentrate on discussing ideas, developing them, criticizing them or opposing them. A strong solidarity between people supporting the same political and social aims, such as transcending racial divisions, can only happen if we trust each other and create a space where we can think for ourselves and decide what to read, to listen to and to discuss. This is one of the reasons why hate speech laws must be opposed, for example. Many of those trying to fight for a better world, where racism no longer exists, do not have much political, social and economic power. They are often denied access to public space or access to media. Hate speech laws do not empower them but create another political barrier for them to overcome. With these hate speech laws, others with already much power in society can have added control over who should speak and what should be discussed. Bigotry is not opposed with censorship but by having the ability to respond to bigotry. Do we really want to make people already at the bottom of society even more powerless? Frederick Douglass, in his 1860 "Plea for Free Speech in Boston," made a very important point when he said: "To suppress free speech is a double wrong, it violates the rights of the hearer as well as those of the speaker." He understood the importance of speech for those fighting for freedom and he made it very clear when he declared:

> Liberty is meaningless where the right to utter one's thoughts and opinions has ceased to exist. That, of all rights, is the dread of tyrants. It is the right which they first of all strike down. They know its power. Thrones, dominions, principalities, and powers, founded in injustice and wrong, are sure to tremble, if men are allowed to reason of righteousness, temperance, and of a judgment to come in their presence. Slavery cannot tolerate free speech.[3]

Since he made that speech, there have been numerous examples showing how fragile this right is and how easily it is taken away from us. People have been attacked, imprisoned or killed for speaking out against tyranny. Excuses such as national security, protecting the innocents and vulnerable people, protecting privacy or fighting bigotry have been presented in order to justify the curtailment of speech.

Of course, those really defending free speech, defined as freedom and power to control one's own life, should also oppose bigotry and injustice. Frederick Douglass supported free speech because it allowed him to oppose slavery and because he understood that black Americans were the ones who would be most likely affected by censorship. He fought for the liberation of black people and freedom of speech can be seen as part of this liberation. However, the claim to support free speech can also be motivated by different political positions and thus have various meanings and motivations. We have already seen different meanings for freedom in the previous chapter. Nevertheless, if the support for free speech is really about freedom, then a basic opposition to what prevents people from being free, situations such as bigotry or social inequalities, is the logical conclusion. But then, some people dispute this and claim that the support for hate speech laws is the right position for those opposing racism.

Some arguments for the support for hate speech laws are based on the notion that hate speech undermines an important sense of security and inclusiveness in the public or collective space. This sense of inclusiveness and security is a public good which is undermined by allowing unregulated hate speech.[4] Jeremy Waldron also interpreted hate speech as "a calculated affront to the dignity of vulnerable members of society." He argued that all "members of society in good standing" are under society's protection and concern and expect to be treated in certain manners. These manners express a basic social standing called "dignity"; and all equal members of society are entitled to have their dignity unaffected. Unrestricted hate speech, for instance publicly insulting some people because of their religion, undermines their dignity. For Jeremy Waldron, the notions of protection and security are what leads him to support some kind of hate speech laws. He is sharing a very commonplace view of individuals as needing the protection of the state and others. Either all members of society are supposed to need protection or sections of the population such as black people are particularly vulnerable and need more protection than others. These ideas of hate speech laws and protection raise many questions. How is hate speech defined? Is speech offending a person's feelings, criticizing another's religion or degrading an individual defined as hate speech? Who defines what is hate speech? The various definitions of hate speech in places where hate speech laws are created already show the difficulty in defining "hate" and "hate speech." Who are the members of society strong enough to protect everybody else? If people are portrayed as vulnerable, are they really expected to be capable of control over their own lives? What happens to freedom when we argue that people need protection?

An anti-racist movement is supposed to be about fighting for freedom and for the power to control individuals' own lives. In what way are they regaining control when they are portrayed as vulnerable people needing protection? The demand for more control over their own lives is what can politically unite an oppressed person with many others who are not necessarily oppressed but still not free. Ordinary people or the working class have very little control over their own lives. And their control is still decreasing today with the growing interference of the state in every aspect of people's lives. New laws, rules and regulations tell people how to behave and live within their family, how to conduct themselves in the most private areas of their lives. Fighting for freedom, for the ability to make their own decisions and act upon these decisions, without the domination of others, is the political aim that unites those who suffered from racial, cultural and economic inequalities, those who are exploited and those who have lost control over their lives. People seen as vulnerable do not get freedom and control but protection. Thus, we cannot support hate speech laws as protection of our dignity and security if we do want to be free and in control. Any argument that is based on the notion of protection is counter-productive in the fight for freedom. Hence, those promoting free speech, but on the grounds that it protects and empowers minorities, are also wrong. They view people the same way as those calling for hate speech laws as protection for minorities.

We can observe this when some supporters of freedom of speech demand laws and regulations to implement it and to punish its opponents.

Additionally, claims of "free speech" without any engagement with the content of speech can often be merely demands for people to stop interacting with each other. Engaging with the ideas of others and opposing them if needs be is essential if people and the principle of free speech are to be taken seriously. It is also important in politics. Otherwise, it becomes a non-judgmental position where we demand to live parallel lives with no intellectual contacts. Censorship does not oppose racist ideas and bigotry and censoring ideas someone does not like is an act of cowardice. It avoids the vital acts of engaging with ideas, developing arguments, opposing the disturbing ideas and convincing others. Supporting free speech without engaging with ideas is an act of cowardice as well. The non-judgmental position hides the refusal to engage with ideas or to oppose racist ideas and bigotry but with an added attempt to give the illusion of support for freedom. Ultimately, respecting other people entails taking their opinions seriously and engaging with their ideas. Ignoring their opinions, accepting their opinions without judgment or simply not taking a moment or a little amount of mental energy to think about what others are saying is not a sign of respect.

Can we form political solidarity with others when our individual autonomy is constantly dismissed and undermined? Ideas, laws and regulations that imagine us incapable of making the rational, the good or right decisions for ourselves, for our family, for the world or for our future have become common. We have seen how humanity is portrayed as causally determined by race, biology, culture, identity or psychology which leaves no room for the influence of human reason. Cause and effect relationships between external factors out of human control and human actions are continuously put forward. There is, for example, an on-going search for psychological and biological roots of political positions and party affiliation. A study tried to suggest that liberals and conservatives do not have the same brain structure.[5] Instead, others suggested a "liberal gene," brain functioning or personality type.[6] The manner in which we understand human nature depends on our political orientations and moral beliefs. At present, the view that human nature is fixed is generally accepted, reflecting the sense of limitations and a lack of hope for the future permeating Western society. The main disagreement is on the definition of this fixed nature. But is it fixed? Can we simply explain racial divisions as an "us and them" attitude, for example? Historical evidence, as we saw in previous chapters, shows that these divisions cannot be explained in this simplistic way. Can we explain the current search for identities as part of a natural human need? Not if we recognize that the notion of the self and notion of the individual as separate from society are historically specific. Larry Siedentop in his book *Inventing the Individual: The Origins of Western Liberalism* took us through a two-thousand year history in an attempt to interpret how, in Western culture, humans have seen themselves as individuals. He argued that Christianity had an important role in developing the individual of liberalism.[7] He is right when we consider the liberal understanding of the individual but, of course, this is not the only way we comprehend ourselves.

Acting on the world changes humanity and the individual. The change in who we are will have effects on the actions taken upon the world. We constantly change ourselves but also our perception of ourselves. An anti-racist movement cannot but oppose philosophies and thoughts that deny human potential in influencing its own destiny. Ideas attacking notions of individual autonomy are political obstacles to anti-racist political action. People must be allowed to think for themselves and be morally responsible for their decisions and actions. This is the opposite view of a racist notion where our thoughts and actions are seen as fully determined by our races or cultures. In the world today, individual autonomy and free speech are political ideals not realities but the support for these ideals will highlight the obstacles preventing people from achieving them. Demands to curtail these ideals because they cannot exist today in a capitalist society do not oppose the difficulties we need to overcome to create a better society but accept them as permanent features human beings cannot surmount. It is a defeatist attitude.

Diversity and Meritocracy: keeping the status quo

The prevalent defeatist attitude we need to overcome if we want to challenge racial thinking and racism can be seen with the issue of diversity, for example. Literary theorist Walter Benn Michaels has noted that "our commitment to diversity has redefined the opposition to discrimination as the appreciation (rather than the elimination) of difference. So with respect to race, the idea is not just that racism is a bad thing (which of course it is) but that race itself is a good thing."[8] Rather than oppose racial thinking and promote social transformation, like radical anti-racists of the past, contemporary demands for better representation and for diversity accept the concept of race. Hence, Michaels described "how antiracism plays an essentially conservative role in American politics today" by showing the contemporary focus on "cultural equality" rather than on "economic equality."[9] This focus, for example, may well hide the reality that, in many contemporary cases, social class has a bigger impact on education achievement than race. The solutions proposed can then be completely inadequate. Alternatively, promoting the myth of meritocracy to challenge these demands for diversity and representation or to oppose the notion of racial thinking is also not an option if we want to transcend racial divisions. It also keeps the status quo. Many argue that rather than choosing people according to their race, culture or identity, they should be selected according to their merit as individuals. Meritocracy is supposed to be a society or political system where individuals have economic, political and social power on the basis of their abilities, talent, effort, performance and achievement. But meritocracy is a concept or a myth, fortunately not a reality. It is also hard to take seriously the belief that meritocracy has ever existed in a society where race, culture, class, religion, nationality, sexuality and gender have had so much influence in people's lives. Every day we are confronted with examples showing how social origins greatly determine the distribution of power and privilege. The place of birth can determine whether one has a good education or no education at all. The wealth of one's parents, class or race influence one's access to the best in health services. But still the myth seems well established for now.

The term itself was coined by sociologist Michael Young in 1958 when he published his satirical essay *The Rise of The Meritocracy*. When published, the book was well received because the concept of meritocracy can help to justify the political, social and economic elites' positions in capitalist society. They want others to believe that they are at the top because they have shown their worth. By implication, those at the bottom of society are those with less value. The notion of the free and right-bearing individual in liberal democracies who simply needs to work hard to succeed helps in keeping the myth alive. Many have forgotten or ignored the fact that Young's essay was a satire "showing how sad, and fragile, a meritocratic society could be."[10] In his dystopian meritocratic society, the cleverest individuals rule society, and people are sorted by the formula I.Q. + effort = merit, creating "not an aristocracy of birth, not a plutocracy of wealth, but a true meritocracy of talent."[11] But, of course, many parents would try to help their kids achieve and those at the top of the meritocracy eventually would use their power to do so, showing the very fragility of meritocracy. Another objection arises when we ask why people, defined as having less merit, should have less material benefits than others. Young answered the question himself and said that:

> Even if it could be demonstrated that ordinary people had less native ability than those selected for high position, that would not mean that they deserved to get less. Being a member of the "lucky sperm club" confers no moral right to advantage. What one is born with, or without, is not of one's own doing.[12]

This point about meritocracy and value is especially relevant today where an individual's character, including IQ and ability to work hard, is still seen as being determined by biology, race, culture or identity. The notion of meritocracy can be used to keep inequalities between different identity groups.

Social origins still very much determine people's lives even with demands of diversity and representations. But as seen with the discussions about Brexit and Trump, the level of education, not aristocratic origins, has become "the primary marker of social difference." Social divisions such as class are currently expressed and justified with levels of education.[13] Society is increasingly seen as divided between the "educated" people who necessarily had access to higher education and the "uneducated" people who are the remaining people. Many essential workers, especially those who are called "unskilled" and "low-skilled" workers, are the lowest-paid workers dealing with terrible working conditions, constantly demonized or forgotten. But for the intellectuals, academics, journalists, stockbrokers, politicians and others to live and thrive, they need the work of these "uneducated people."

Anti-political approach

One of the main points I wanted to highlight in the book was the anti-political aspect of the current notions of race, culture and politicized identities. I think a human world with no politics is a purposeless and meaningless world where humanity has given up on the ambition of creating a freer world and has lost a sense of possibility in their actions. The growth in politicized identities greatly damages the political realm and alarmingly reduces the possibilities for political solidarities. This is one of the most critical consequences for an anti-racism movement. If we are all separated by fixed identities and if these identities are used to fight for particular interests against all other identities' interests, we have no longer any common ground, common interests and common goals with others.[14] A common goal which recognized the importance of challenging racial thinking and racism has been turned into competitions between different racial, ethnic and cultural identities. Each of these identities is competing in showing how they have suffered and are still suffering in order to have their demands accepted as priorities compared to the others' demands. More material resources given to the Mexicans, African Americans, Afro-Caribbeans or to the white working class?

Identity as victim has become the tactic to claim authority over others in a world where vulnerability is one of the main descriptions applied to humanity. And of course, the other description is wickedness which creates the victims. In our current culture, deeds and accidents against an individual are seen as more important than the actions and decisions of an individual. It has become hard for those who refuse to be seen as permanent victims. Samantha Geimer, the 13-year-old girl raped by Roman Polanski 43 years ago, refuses to be seen as a traumatized victim but it seems that her opinion does not matter much in the continuous Polanski story. In 2013, she wrote a memoir, *The Girl: Life in the Shadow of Roman Polanski*, explaining her own attitude of forgiveness toward the experience. Years ago, she was the victim of wrongdoing, of an act considered morally wrong today but is it right to try and force her to see herself as a traumatized girl throughout her whole life, to try and force her to adopt a victim mentality?[15]

There are better reasons than terrible personal experiences to recognize the importance of opposing racial thinking and racism. Opposing social barriers in the fight for human emancipation is a political aim worth fighting for and even dying for as so many have done in the past. One day, I hope, human beings will build a world where the majority of humanity will be able to develop their own individuality and able to participate fully in society, regardless of their skin color, ethnicity, gender, sexuality or religion. That is why the oppression, discrimination and other social barriers that prevent ordinary people from enjoying what humanity has already understood and accomplished are essential political issues that need to be considered at the moment. The universalist and humanist approach of the past radical left movements is the crucial outlook that has been rejected by the last few generations but is also what needs to be urgently redeveloped now. Identity politics, based on anti-universalist ideas, creates divisions when solidarity with others is urgently needed. It is not a coincidence that the ruling elites, the upper classes and cultural elites like Hollywood, part of the American film industry, are very keen on identity politics because, like racism in the past, it is a useful tool to mostly keep how things stand. Some of the most privileged people on the planet can perform, feel guilty about groups of people and declare support for a few individuals to join their ranks. Then they can carry on as before, leaving the majority of people struggling at the bottom and dealing with the same social problems. The use of politicized identities is a tool for the middle-class individuals trying to access the top of society. It is not a fight to create a free society where people would no longer be judged and condemned because of their race, ethnicity or culture.

A poor black worker may be happy to see a black person recognized as a great author because of the hope it represents.

He may hope that the public recognition of this other black person means that the social barriers faced by black people are disappearing and that, one day, being black would be no more a barrier to equal opportunities and equal access. But the public recognition of the author, in itself, is not challenging the social barriers faced by black people for being black and certainly not the social barriers faced by the poor and working-class people. In fact, the constant focus on the race issue and relentless racialization of all social issues hides the divisions and differential interests between classes. Black people are portrayed as a classless group with common economic and political interests. This is, of course, a very useful argument for the black middle classes and upper classes who can use the problems faced by poor black people to build the notion of victimhood for the whole group. A black worker is now supposed to feel better with a black employer than a white employer according to this focus on race. Since when are low wages and/or bad working conditions easier to accept from a black employer than if they were coming from a white employer? Are they not asking for equality in the right to exploit others? We can see how constant loud claims of racism are currently useful for many black and white activists, in the West, who often come from the most privileged classes, from the educated middle class and upper class. The radical notion that, in order to challenge racism, the capitalist social organization had to be challenged and transformed, has been mostly rejected at the moment. The claims of racism today are often to highlight the perceived disadvantages a group is encountering and to demand reparations, extra benefits, privileges and actions from society and from others. When funds for black entrepreneurs are demanded and accepted, for example, it is celebrated as an anti-racist win. But is it? Who benefits from these gains? The poor black workers, together with their poor white neighbors, will still be struggling to pay their bills, while the black entrepreneurs will be making better deals with the white entrepreneurs. Society would still be the same with much inequality but with a more racially and culturally diverse privileged minority at the top of the social ladder. Essentially, politics and freedom have been removed from contemporary identity-based anti-racism.

Utopian thinking

Alternatively, in politics, utopian thinking or thinking in possibilities involves recognizing the active and subjective nature of humanity. Humanity's decisions and actions and their consequences are seen as partly unpredictable. This unpredictability is based on the use of our reason, on our rejection of "impossibility" and on our search for possibilities. This approach leads us to see the future as open-ended. South-African academic Richard Turner argued that "(c)ommon-sense thinking obscures reality" because it does not lead us to ask questions about the way we currently live. The present seems more permanent than as part of history. Thus, Turner argued for the importance of utopian thinking because unless "we can see our society in the light of other possible societies we cannot even understand how and why it works as it does, let alone judge it."[16] To accept the open-endedness of the future is to accept uncertainty as a natural part of the human condition. Jean-Paul Sartre, one of the key figures in existentialist thoughts, suggested that we "are left alone, without excuse," explaining "that man is condemned to be free. Condemned, because he did not create himself, yet is nevertheless at liberty, and from the moment that he is thrown into this world he is responsible for everything he does."[17] Without God and a fixed human nature making decisions for him, a rational individual makes his own choices and in good faith, should accept responsibility for these choices. But, according to Sartre, human beings are afraid of this freedom. It seems that they want identities, ancestors, traditions, histories, nature and others to make decisions for them.

In a society where hierarchy and order were understood

as given by God and/or nature, certainty was an important feature of the cultural life. People knew their place and role in life because it was already assigned to them from birth or from tradition. The Renaissance humanists, Enlightenment humanists and radical humanists such as Karl Marx put human beings as the subject of history, not just as an object acted upon by external forces. They recognized humanity's defining features in their reason, transformative action, creative ability and future-oriented power. They recognized that human consciousness can have a decisive role in shaping history and rejected fatalistic beliefs. This recognition inevitably leads to understanding that uncertainty is part of the human condition.

In *Man's Search for Meaning*, Viktor E Frankl discussed life in Nazi death camps and argued that, ultimately, the individual makes his own decisions on how to act even when faced with terrible situations. People in horrendous situations can still act with compassion or selfishness, show solidarity with others or try to save their own life at all cost to others. Thus, Frankl reminded us that "everything can be taken from a man but one thing: the last of the human freedoms – to choose one's attitude in any given set of circumstances, to choose one's own way."[18] The notion of individual responsibility is important but it is only right if it also recognizes that human beings are social beings and not only isolated individuals living within a community of isolated individuals. Our individuality, moral values, meaning of life, sense of limitation or of hope are developed through others, through society. We can recognize an individual's autonomy in making decisions but understand this as a product of human social development. Thus, this understanding of individuals' ultimate responsibility should also be considered when we discuss political groups or humanity as a whole. Humanity or political groups, in their struggle to survive while facing natural and social laws, are ultimately responsible for their decisions and actions. These decisions include passively accepting being dominated by external forces or understanding these forces in order to bend, change, overcome or destroy them. An effective anti-racist movement will have to be a political, universalist and humanist movement fighting for freedom, for a freer society where we all refuse the destructive domination of race, ethnicity and culture over our decisions and our actions.

Endnotes

Introduction

1 Arendt, Hannah and Kohn, Jerome (2018) *Thinking without a banister: essays in understanding, 1953-1975* First Edition., Schocken Books, New York, Schocken Books, p. 498.

2 Anon (2018) "Cartoonist suspends Twitter account amid Serena Williams backlash." *Herald Sun,* September 12. [online] Available from: https://www.heraldsun.com.au/sport/tennis/herald-sun-backs-mark-knights-cartoon-on-serena-williams/news-story/594b06bcafa578d667f679e490b85091

3 Guy-Sheftall, Beverly (ed.) (1995) *Words of fire: an anthology of African-American feminist thought,* New York, New Press: Distributed by W.W. Norton.

Chapter 1

1 DiAngelo, Robin J. (2018) *White fragility: why it's so hard for white people to talk about racism,* Boston, Beacon Press.

2 Miles, Robert (1993) *Racism after "race relations,"* London; New York, Routledge.

3 Barkan, Elazar (1992) *The retreat of scientific racism: changing concepts of race in Britain and the United States between the world wars,* Cambridge; New York, Cambridge University Press.

4 Malik, Kenan (1996) *The meaning of race: race, history and culture in Western society,* Basingstoke, Hampshire, Macmillan.

5 Barkan, Elazar (1992) *The retreat of scientific racism.*

6 Kendi, Ibram X. (2017) *Stamped from the beginning: the definitive history of racist ideas in America,* London, The Bodley Head.

7 Kendi, Ibram X. (2017) *Stamped from the beginning.*

8   Furedi, Frank (1992) *Mythical past, elusive future: history and society in an anxious age*, London; Concord, Mass, Pluto Press, p. 62.

9   Alexander, Inigo (2019) "Now 90% of England agrees: being English is not about colour." *The Guardian*, June 30. [online] Available from: https://www.theguardian.com/society/2019/jun/30/being-english-not-about-colour-say-majority

10   Malik, Kenan (1996) *The meaning of race.*

11   Wood, Ellen Meiksins (2008) *Citizens to lords: a social history of western political thought from antiquity to the Middle Ages*, London; New York, Verso.

12   Wood, Ellen Meiksins (2008) *Citizens to lords.*

13   Hannaford, Ivan (1996) *Race: the history of an idea in the West*, Washington, D.C.: Baltimore, Md, Woodrow Wilson Center Press; Order from the Johns Hopkins University Press.

14   Snowden, Jr, Frank M. (1948) "The Negro in Ancient Greece." *American Anthropologist*, 50(1), pp. 31–44.

15   Snowden, Frank M. (1970) *Blacks in Antiquity: Ethiopians in the Greco-Roman experience*, Cambridge, Mass. [u.a.], Belknap Press of Harvard Univ. Press.

16   Malik, Kenan (2014) *The quest for a moral compass: a global history of ethics*, London, Atlantic Books.

17   Hannaford, Ivan (1996) *Race: the history of an idea in the West.*

18   Hannaford, Ivan (1996) *Race: the history of an idea in the West.*

19   Gossett, Thomas F. (1997) *Race: The history of an idea in America* New ed., New York, NY [u.a.], Oxford Univ. Press.

20   Gossett, Thomas F. (1997) *Race: The history of an idea in America.*

21   Hannaford, Ivan (1996) *Race: the history of an idea in the West.*

22   Todorov, Tzvetan (1994) *On human diversity: nationalism, racism, and exoticism in French thought* 2. print., Cambridge, Mass, Harvard Univ. Press.

23   Pagden, Anthony (2015) *The enlightenment and why it still*

matters 1st publ. in paperback., Oxford, Oxford Univ. Press.

24 Pagden, Anthony (2015) *The enlightenment and why it still matters.*

25 Gossett, Thomas F. (1997) *Race the history of an idea in America.*

26 Hannaford, Ivan (1996) *Race: the history of an idea in the West.*

27 Todorov, Tzvetan (1994) *On human diversity.*

28 Todorov, Tzvetan (1994) *On human diversity.*

29 Gossett, Thomas F. (1997) *Race the history of an idea in America.*

30 Berlin, Ira (2018) *The long emancipation: the demise of slavery in the United States,* Cambridge, Mass, Harvard Univ. Press

31 Hannaford, Ivan (1996) *Race: the history of an idea in the West.*

32 Todorov, Tzvetan (1994) *On human diversity.*

33 Gossett, Thomas F. (1997) *Race the history of an idea in America.*

34 Gossett, Thomas F. (1997) *Race the history of an idea in America.*

35 Gossett, Thomas F. (1997) *Race the history of an idea in America.*

36 Malik, Kenan (2008) *Strange fruit: why both sides are wrong in the race debate,* Oxford, Oneworld.

37 Gossett, Thomas F. (1997) *Race the history of an idea in America.*

38 Henry, John (2012) *A short history of scientific thought,* Houndmills, Basingstoke, Hampshire; New York, Palgrave Macmillan.

39 Henry, John (2012) *A short history of scientific thought.*

40 Malik, Kenan (1996) *The meaning of race.*

41 Hannaford, Ivan (1996) *Race: the history of an idea in the West.*

42 Jones, Greta (1980) *Social Darwinism and English thought: the interaction between biological and social theory,* Brighton, Harvester Pr. p. 145.

43 Hannaford, Ivan (1996) *Race: the history of an idea in the West.*

44 Hannaford, Ivan (1996) *Race: the history of an idea in the West.*

45 Arendt, Hannah (1973) *The origins of totalitarianism* New ed., New York, Harcourt Brace Jovanovich.

46 Todorov, Tzvetan (1994) *On human diversity.*

47 Todorov, Tzvetan (1994) *On human diversity.*

48 Williams, Eric (1944) *Capitalism and Slavery*, Chapel Hill, North Carolina Univ. Press, Scholar Select published by Andesite Press.

49 Williams, Eric (1944) *Capitalism and Slavery*, p. 7.

50 Williams, Eric (1944) *Capitalism and Slavery.*

51 Allen, Theodore (2012) *The invention of the white race* Second edition, London; New York, Verso.

52 Allen, Theodore (2012) *The invention of the white race.*

53 Allen, Theodore (2012) *The invention of the white race.*

54 Malik, Kenan (1996) *The meaning of race.*

55 Hobsbawm, Eric John (1995) *The age of revolution Europe 1789-1848* reprint., London, Abacus.

56 Israel, Jonathan I. (2014) *Revolutionary ideas: an intellectual history of the French Revolution from the Rights of Man to Robespierre*, Oxford; Princeton, New Jersey, Princeton University Press.

57 Hobsbawm, Eric John (1995) *The age of revolution Europe 1789-1848.*

58 Israel, Jonathan I. (2014) *Revolutionary ideas.*

59 Malik, Kenan (1996) *The meaning of race*, p. 69.

60 Israel, Jonathan I. (2014) *Revolutionary ideas.*

61 Israel, Jonathan I. (2014) *Revolutionary ideas.*

62 Malik, Kenan (1996) *The meaning of race.*

Chapter 2

1 Todorov, Tzvetan (1994) *On human diversity: nationalism, racism, and exoticism in French thought* 2. print., Cambridge, Mass, Harvard Univ. Press.

2 Marx, Karl and Engels, Frederick (n.d.) *Karl Marx and*

Frederick Engels: Selected Works in one volume, Lawrence & Wishart.

3   Hannaford, Ivan (1996) *Race: the history of an idea in the West*, Washington, D.C.: Baltimore, Md, Woodrow Wilson Center Press; Order from the Johns Hopkins University Press.

4   Bouie, Jamelle (2018) "The Enlightenment's Dark Side." *Slate*, June 5. [online] Available from: https://slate.com/news-and-politics/2018/06/taking-the-enlightenment-seriously-requires-talking-about-race.html

5   Mill, John Stuart (1993) *On liberty and Utilitarianism*, New York, Bantam Books, p. 45.

6   Kant, Immanuel (2009) *An answer to the question: "what is enlightenment?,"* London; New York, Penguin Books, p. 1.

7   Pagden, Anthony (2015) *The enlightenment and why it still matters* 1st publ. in paperback., Oxford, Oxford Univ. Press.

8   Israel, Jonathan (2017) *The expanding blaze: how the American Revolution ignited the world, 1775-1848*, Princeton; Oxford, Princeton University Press.

9   Marx, Karl and Engels, Frederick (n.d.) *Selected Works in one volume*.

10 Luther King, Jr, Martin (n.d.) "'I have a dream...' speech." [online] Available from: https://www.archives.gov/files/press/exhibits/dream-speech.pdf

11 Anon (2016) "Gorilla killing: Harambe's death at zoo prompts backlash." *BBC.com*, May 30. [online] Available from: https://www.bbc.com/news/world-us-canada-36410841

12 Malik, Kenan (1996) *The meaning of race: race, history and culture in Western society*, Basingstoke, Hampshire, Macmillan.

13 Thiesse, Anne-Marie (2001) *La création des identités nationales: Europe, XVIIIe-XXe siècle*, Paris, Editions du Seuil.

14 Thiesse, Anne-Marie (2001) *La création des identités nationales*.

15 Hannaford, Ivan (1996) *Race: the history of an idea in the West*.

16 Finkielkraut, Alain and Mazal Holocaust Collection (1995)

The defeat of the mind, New York, Columbia University Press.

17 Thiesse, Anne-Marie (2001) *La création des identités nationales*.

18 Malik, Kenan (1996) *The meaning of race*.

19 Kyriakides, Christopher and Torres, Rodolfo D. (2012) *Race defaced: paradigms of pessimism, politics of possibility*, Stanford, California, Stanford University Press.

20 Noiriel, Gérard (2015) *Qu'est-ce qu'une nation? le "vivre ensemble" à la française: réflexions d'un historien*, Montrouge, Bayard.

21 Noiriel, Gérard (2015) *Qu'est-ce qu'une nation? le "vivre ensemble" à la française*.

22 Hobsbawm, E. J. (1992) *Nations and nationalism since 1780: programme, myth, reality* 2nd ed., Cambridge [England]; New York, Cambridge University Press, p. 20.

23 Silverman, Maxim (2014) *Deconstructing the nation: immigration, racism and citizenship in modern France* First issued in paperback 2014., London New York, Routledge, p. 27.

24 Finkielkraut, Alain and Mazal Holocaust Collection (1995) *The defeat of the mind*.

25 Hannaford, Ivan (1996) *Race: the history of an idea in the West*.

26 Hobsbawm, E. J. (1992) *Nations and nationalism since 1780*.

27 Todorov, Tzvetan (1994) *On human diversity*.

28 Todorov, Tzvetan (1994) *On human diversity*.

29 Todorov, Tzvetan (1994) *On human diversity*.

30 Malik, Kenan (1996) *The meaning of race*.

31 Hobsbawm, Eric John (1995) *The age of revolution Europe 1789-1848* reprint., London, Abacus.

32 Jones, Greta (1980) *Social Darwinism and English thought: the interaction between biological and social theory*, Brighton, Harvester Pr. [u.a.].

33 Kühl, Stefan (2002) *The Nazi Connection: eugenics, American racism, and German national socialism*, New York, Oxford University Press.

34 Jones, Greta (1980) *Social Darwinism and English thought.*

35 Kühl, Stefan (2002) *The Nazi Connection.*

36 Kyriakides, Christopher and Torres, Rodolfo D. (2012) *Race deface, p. 72.*

37 Furedi, Frank (1998) *The silent war: imperialism and the changing perception of race,* London, Pluto Press.

38 Furedi, Frank (1998) *The silent war.*

39 Barkan, Elazar (1992) *The retreat of scientific racism: changing concepts of race in Britain and the United States between the world wars,* Cambridge; New York, Cambridge University Press.

40 Kühl, Stefan (2002) *The Nazi Connection.*

41 Kühl, Stefan (2002) *The Nazi Connection, p. 38.*

42 Kühl, Stefan (2002) *The Nazi Connection.*

43 Kühl, Stefan (2002) *The Nazi Connection.*

44 Degler, Carl N. (1991) *In search of human nature: the decline and revival of Darwinism in American social thought,* New York, Oxford University Press.

45 Vermette, David (2019) "When an Influx of French-Canadian Immigrants Struck Fear into Americans." *Smithsonian.com,* August 21. [online] Available from: https://www.smithsonianmag.com/history/french-canadian-immigrants-struck-fear-into-new-england-communities-180972951/

46 Silverman, Maxim (2014) *Deconstructing the nation.*

47 Denselow, Robin (2019) "Johnny Clegg obituary." *The Guardian,* July 19. [online] Available from: https://www.theguardian.com/music/2019/jul/19/johnny-clegg-obituary

48 Oluo, Ijeoma (2018) *So you want to talk about race* First edition., New York, NY, Seal Press.

49 Anon (2016) "Whose life is it anyway? Novelists have their say on cultural appropriation," *The Guardian,* October 1. [online] Available from: https://www.theguardian.com/books/2016/oct/01/novelists-cultural-appropriation-

literature-lionel-shriver

50 Todorov, Tzvetan (1994) *On human diversity.*

51 Todorov, Tzvetan (1994) *On human diversity.*

52 Todorov, Tzvetan (1994) *On human diversity.*

53 Oluo, Ijeoma (2018) *So you want to talk about race.*

54 Eddo-Lodge, Reni (2018) *Why I'm no longer talking to white people about race* Expanded edition., London Oxford New York New Delhi Sydney, Bloomsbury Publishing.

55 Fanon, Frantz, (2002) *Les damnés de la terre (1961),* Preface: Sartre, Jean-Paul (1961), Cherki, Alice (2002) and postface: Harbi, Mohammed (2002), 75013 Paris, La Decouverte

56 Taylor, Jeremy (2009) *Not a chimp: the hunt to find the genes that make us human,* Oxford; New York, Oxford University Press.

57 Tallis, Raymond (2012) *Aping mankind: neuromania, Darwinitis and the misrepresentation of humanity* 1st pbk. ed., Durham [England], Acumen Pub, p. 8.

58 Malik, Kenan (1996) *The meaning of race.*

59 Malik, Kenan (1996) *The meaning of race, p. 151.*

60 Malik, Kenan (1996) *The meaning of race.*

61 Monaghan, John and Just, Peter (2000) *Social and cultural anthropology: a very short introduction,* Oxford [England] New York, Oxford University Press.

62 Degler, Carl N. (1991) *In search of human nature.*

63 Degler, Carl N. (1991) *In search of human nature.*

64 Malik, Kenan (2000) *Man, beast and zombie: what science can and cannot tell us about human nature,* London, Weidenfeld & Nicolson.

65 Malik, Kenan (2000) *Man, beast and zombie.*

66 Sellars, Kirsten (2002) *The rise and rise of human rights,* Stroud, Gloucestershire, Sutton.

67 Anon (1945) "UNESCO Constitution." *UNESCO.org.* [online] Available from: http://portal.unesco.org/en/ev.php-URL_ ID=15244&URL_DO=DO_TOPIC&URL_SECTION=201.

html

68 UNESCO Paris (1952) *The Race Concept. The Race Question in Modern Science. Results of an Inquiry*, Paris, Imprimerie des Arts et Manufactures.

69 UNESCO Paris (1952) *The Race Concept.*

70 UNESCO Paris (1952) *The Race Concept.*

71 UNESCO (1950) "The Race Question."

72 UNESCO (1950) "The Race Question."

73 UNESCO (1950) "The Race Question."

74 Carey, John (1992) *The intellectuals and the masses: pride and prejudice among the literary intelligentsia, 1880-1939*, London, Faber and Faber.

75 UNESCO Paris (1952) *The Race Concept.*

76 Degler, Carl N. (1991) *In search of human nature.*

77 Fisher, Mark (2009) *Capitalist realism: is there no alternative?* Winchester, O Books.

78 Fisher, Mark (2009) *Capitalist realism: is there no alternative?*

79 Mill, John Stuart and Mill, John Stuart (1993) *On liberty.*

Chapter 3

1 Izenberg, Gerald (2016) *Identity: the necessity of a modern idea* 1st edition., Philadelphia, University of Pennsylvania Press.

2 Gleason, Philip (1983) "Identifying Identity: A Semantic History." *The Journal of American History*, 69(4), p. 910. [online] Available from: https://academic.oup.com/jah/article-lookup/doi/10.2307/1901196 (Accessed February 21, 2020).

3 Gleason, Philip (1983) "Identifying Identity: A Semantic History."

4 Izenberg, Gerald (2016) *Identity: the necessity of a modern idea.*

5 Izenberg, Gerald (2016) *Identity: the necessity of a modern idea.*

6 Moran, Marie (2015) *Identity and capitalism*, Los Angeles,

SAGE.

7   Izenberg, Gerald (2016) *Identity: the necessity of a modern idea.*

8   Gleason, Philip (1983) "Identifying Identity: A Semantic History."

9   Erikson, Erik H. (1995) *Childhood and society* Rev. ed., London, Vintage.

10 Moskowitz, Eva S. (2001) *In therapy we trust: America's obsession with self-fulfillment,* Baltimore, Johns Hopkins University Press.

11 Bracken, Patrick (2003) *Trauma: culture, meaning, and philosophy,* London Philadelphia, Whurr, p. 7.

12 Bracken, Patrick (2003) *Trauma: culture, meaning, and philosophy.*

13 Moran, Marie (2015) *Identity and capitalism.*

14 Moran, Marie (2015) *Identity and capitalism.*

15 Arendt, Hannah (2006) *Eichmann in Jerusalem: a report on the banality of evil,* New York, N.Y, Penguin Books.

16 Noiriel, Gérard (2007) *À quoi sert 'l'identité nationale',* Marseille, Agone.

17 Churchwell, Sarah (2019) "America's Original Identity Politics." *The New York Review of Books,* February 7. [online] Available from: https://www.nybooks.com/daily/2019/02/07/americas-original-identity-politics/

18 DiAngelo, Robin (2011) "White Fragility." *International Journal of Critical Pedagogy,* Vol 3(3), pp. 54–70.

19 Mészáros, István (2006) *Marx's theory of alienation,* London, Merlin Press, p. 80.

20 Mészáros, István (2006) *Marx's theory of alienation.*

21 Marx, Karl and Engels, Frederick (n.d.) *Karl Marx and Frederick Engels: Selected Works in one volume,* Lawrence & Wishart, p. 181.

22 Marx, Karl and Engels, Frederick (n.d.) *Selected Works in one volume.*

23 Steele, Shelby (2007) *White guilt: how blacks and whites together destroyed the promise of the civil rights era*, New York [u.a], Harper Perennial.

24 Gillott, John and Kumar, Manjit (1995) *Science and the retreat from reason*, London, Merlin Press.

25 Gillott, John and Kumar, Manjit (1995) *Science and the retreat from reason*.

26 Gillott, John and Kumar, Manjit (1995) *Science and the retreat from reason*.

27 Furedi, Frank (1986) *The Soviet Union demystified: a materialist analysis*, London, Junius.

28 Furedi, Frank (1986) *The Soviet Union demystified*.

29 Kyriakides, Christopher and Torres, Rodolfo D. (2012) *Race defaced: paradigms of pessimism, politics of possibility*, Stanford, California, Stanford University Press.

30 Kyriakides, Christopher and Torres, Rodolfo D. (2012) *Race defaced*.

31 Sabine, George H. (1950) *A History of Political Theory* Revised Edition., New York, Henry Holt and Company, Inc.

32 Wolin, Sheldon S. (2016) *Politics and vision: continuity and innovation in Western political thought* Princeton Classics edition, Expanded edition., Princeton, Princeton University Press.

33 Sabine, George H. (1950) *A History of Political Theory*.

34 Wolin, Sheldon S. (2016) *Politics and vision*.

35 Russell, Bertrand (1995) *History of Western Philosophy and its connection with political and social circumstances from the earliest times to the present day* Reprinted., London, Routledge.

36 Wolin, Sheldon S. (2016) *Politics and vision*.

37 Israel, Jonathan (2017) *The expanding blaze: how the American Revolution ignited the world, 1775-1848*, Princeton; Oxford, Princeton University Press.

38 Sabine, George H. (1950) *A History of Political Theory*.

39 Pettit, Philip (2014) *Just freedom: a moral compass for a complex world* First Edition., New York, W.W. Norton & Company.

40 Pettit, Philip (2014) *Just freedom: a moral compass for a complex world.*

41 Sabine, George H. (1950) *A History of Political Theory.*

42 Wolin, Sheldon S. (2016) *Politics and vision.*

43 Sabine, George H. (1950) *A History of Political Theory.*

44 Malik, Kenan (2014) *The quest for a moral compass: a global history of ethics*, London, Atlantic Books.

45 Wolin, Sheldon S. (2016) *Politics and vision.*

46 Forrester, Katrina (2019) "The Future of Political Philosophy." *Boston Review*, 17 September. [online] Available from: http://bostonreview.net/philosophy-religion/katrina-forrester-future-political-philosophy

47 Wolin, Sheldon S. (2016) *Politics and vision.*

48 Forrester, Katrina (2019) "The Future of Political Philosophy."

49 Heartfield, James (2002) *The "Death of the Subject" Explained*, Sheffield, Sheffield Hallam University Press.

50 Anderson, Perry (1987) *Considerations on Western Marxism* 3. Impression., London, Verso.

51 Anderson, Perry (1987) *Considerations on Western Marxism.*

52 Furedi, Frank (1986) *The Soviet Union demystified*, p. 250.

53 Anderson, Perry (1987) *Considerations on Western Marxism.*

54 Marcuse, Herbert and Kellner, Douglas (2007) *One-dimensional man: studies in the ideology of advanced industrial society* Repr., London, Routledge.

55 Hayden, Tom (1962) "The Port Huron Statement." [online] Available from: http://www.progressivefox.com/misc_documents/PortHuronStatement.pdf

56 Heartfield, James (2002) *The "Death of the Subject" Explained.*

57 Marx, Karl (n.d.) *Capital: A Critique of Political Economy. Volume III The Process of Capitalist Production as a Whole* Engels, F. (ed.), London, Lawrence & Wishart.

58 Furedi, Frank (1986) *The Soviet Union demystified*, p. 8.

59 Mészáros, István (2006) *Marx's theory of alienation*.

60 Lebron, Christopher J. (2017) *The making of Black lives matter: a brief history of an idea*, New York, NY, Oxford University Press.

61 Hannaford, Ivan (1996) *Race: the history of an idea in the West*, Washington, D.C.: Baltimore, Md, Woodrow Wilson Center Press; Order from the Johns Hopkins University Press.

62 Furedi, Frank (2004) *Therapy culture: cultivating vulnerability in an uncertain age*, London; New York, Routledge.

63 Furedi, Frank (2004) *Therapy culture.*

64 Lasch-Quinn, Elisabeth (2002) *Race experts: how racial etiquette, sensitivity training, and new age therapy hijacked the civil rights revolution*, Lanham, Md., Rowman & Littlefield.

65 Mészáros, István (2006) *Marx's theory of alienation*.

66 Arendt, Hannah and Kohn, Jerome (2018) *Thinking without a banister: essays in understanding, 1953-1975* First Edition., Schocken Books, New York, Schocken Books.

67 Taylor, Ros (2019) "Social divisions, toxicity and the future." *Blogs.lse.ac.uk.* [online] Available from: https://blogs.lse.ac.uk/brexit/2019/09/06/categories-stereotypes-and-political-identities-the-use-of-brexiter-and-remainer-in-online-comments/

68 Guy-Sheftall, Beverly (ed.) (1995) *Words of fire: an anthology of African-American feminist thought*, New York, New Press: Distributed by W.W. Norton.

69 Guy-Sheftall, Beverly (ed.) (1995) *Words of fire.*

70 Gordon, Leah N (2016) *From power to prejudice: the rise of racial individualism in midcentury America.* Chicago, Chicago University Press, p. 2.

71 Lasch-Quinn, Elisabeth (2002) *Race experts.*

72 Lasch-Quinn, Elisabeth (2002) *Race experts, p. 132.*

73 Steele, Shelby (2007) *White guilt, p. 34.*

74 Rustin, Bayard, Carbado, Devon W. and Weise, Donald

(2003) *Time on two crosses: the collected writings of Bayard Rustin* 1st ed., San Francisco, Cleis Press.

75 Kyriakides, Christopher and Torres, Rodolfo D. (2012) *Race defaced.*

76 Wolin, Sheldon S. (2016) *Politics and vision.*

77 Arendt, Hannah and Kohn, Jerome (2018) *Thinking without a banister.*

78 Wolin, Sheldon S. (2016) *Politics and vision.*

79 Lukes, Steven (2006) *Individualism*, Colchester, ECPR Press.

80 Wolin, Sheldon S. (2016) *Politics and vision.*

81 Delgado, Richard and Stefancic, Jean (2017) *Critical race theory: an introduction* Third edition., New York, New York University Press.

82 Delgado, Richard and Stefancic, Jean (2017) *Critical race theory: an introduction.*

83 Stockman, Farah (2019) "'We're Self-Interested': The Growing Identity Debate in Black America." *The New York Times*, November 8. [online] Available from: https://www. nytimes.com/2019/11/08/us/slavery-black-immigrants-ados.html

84 K., Marley (2019) "How Did the Holocaust Supersede American Genocide and Slavery?" *Medium*, August 10. [online] Available from: https://medium.com/marleyisms/ how-did-the-jewish-holocaust-supersede-american-genocide-and-slavery-872a6cdabba2

Conclusion

1 Rustin, Bayard, Carbado, Devon W. and Weise, Donald (2003) *Time on two crosses: the collected writings of Bayard Rustin* 1st ed., San Francisco, Cleis Press.

2 Fisher, Mark (2013) "Existing the Vampire Castle." *OpenDemocracyUK.* [online] Available from: https:// www.opendemocracy.net/en/opendemocracyuk/exiting-vampire-castle/?fbclid=IwAR0ArLjlQfLlxwTD4kVPFpw

5N8-o7QbZXUKhavuFSGX4-sE8_KqF5YUbw5w

3   Douglass, Frederick (1860) "Plea for Free Speech in Boston." *Frederick Douglass Papers.* [online] Available from: https://frederickdouglass.infoset.io/islandora/object/islandora:2129#page/1/mode/1up

4   Waldron, Jeremy (2014) *The harm in hate speech* First Harvard University Press paperback edition., Cambridge, Massachusetts London, England, Harvard University Press.

5   Kanai, Ryota, Feilden, Tom, Firth, Colin and Rees, Geraint (2011) "Political orientations are correlated with brain structure in young adults." *Current biology: CB*, 21(8), pp. 677–680.

6   Ninh, Amie (2011) "Liberal vs. Conservative: Does the Difference Lie in the Brain?" *Time*, April 8. [online] Available from: https://healthland.time.com/2011/04/08/liberal-vs-conservative-does-the-difference-lie-in-the-brain/

7   Siedentop, Larry (2015) *Inventing the Individual the origins of western liberalism*, London [u.a.], Penguin Books.

8   Michaels, Walter Benn (2016) *The trouble with diversity how we learned to love identity and ignore inequality* Tenth anniversary edition, first Picador edition., New York, Picador.

9   Michaels, Walter Benn (2016) *The trouble with diversity.*

10   Young, Michael Dunlop (1994) *The rise of the meritocracy*, New Brunswick, N.J., U.S.A, Transaction Publishers.

11   Young, Michael Dunlop (1994) *The rise of the meritocracy.*

12   Young, Michael Dunlop (1994) *The rise of the meritocracy*, p. XVI

13   Malik, Kenan (2018) "Posh is so passe - today's elites prefers the myth of the meritocracy." *The Guardian*, December 30. [online] Available from: https://www.theguardian.com/commentisfree/2018/dec/30/posh-is-so-passe-todays-elite-prefers-the-myth-of-meritocracy

14   Louis-Dit-Sully, Christine (2017) "Return Political Conversation to Principles, Not Identities." *Conatusnews.*

[online] Available from: https://conatusnews.com/political-principles-identities/

15 Keegan, Rebecca (2013) "Samantha Geimer tells her side of story in Roman Polanski case." *Los Angeles Times*, September 16. [online] Available from: https://www.latimes.com/entertainment/la-xpm-2013-sep-16-la-et-jc-geimer-book-20130916-story.html

16 Turner, Richard (1972) "The Eye of the Needle by Rick Turner." *South African History Online*. [online] Available from: https://www.sahistory.org.za/archive/eye-needle-rick-turner

17 Kaufmann, Walter (ed.) (1966) *Existentialism from Dostoevsky to Sartre*, Cleveland,Ohio, Meridian Books, The World Publishing Company.

18 Frankl, Viktor Emil (2006) *Man's search for meaning* Mini book ed., Boston, Beacon Press.

CULTURE, SOCIETY & POLITICS

The modern world is at an impasse. Disasters scroll across our smartphone screens and we're invited to like, follow or upvote, but critical thinking is harder and harder to find. Rather than connecting us in common struggle and debate, the internet has sped up and deepened a long-standing process of alienation and atomization. Zer0 Books wants to work against this trend. With critical theory as our jumping off point, we aim to publish books that make our readers uncomfortable. We want to move beyond received opinions.

Zer0 Books is on the left and wants to reinvent the left. We are sick of the injustice, the suffering, and the stupidity that defines both our political and cultural world, and we aim to find a new foundation for a new struggle.

If this book has helped you to clarify an idea, solve a problem or extend your knowledge, you may want to check out our online content as well. Look for Zer0 Books: Advancing Conversations in the iTunes directory and for our Zer0 Books YouTube channel.

Popular videos include:
Žižek and the Double Blackmain
The Intellectual Dark Web is a Bad Sign
Can there be an Anti-SJW Left?
Answering Jordan Peterson on Marxism

Follow us on Facebook
at https://www.facebook.com/ZeroBooks and Twitter at https://twitter.com/Zer0Books

Bestsellers from Zer0 Books include:

Give Them an Argument
Logic for the Left
Ben Burgis
Many serious leftists have learned to distrust talk of logic. This is a serious mistake.
Paperback: 978-1-78904-210-8 ebook: 978-1-78904-211-5

Poor but Sexy
Culture Clashes in Europe East and West
Agata Pyzik
How the East stayed East and the West stayed West.
Paperback: 978-1-78099-394-2 ebook: 978-1-78099-395-9

An Anthropology of Nothing in Particular
Martin Demant Frederiksen
A journey into the social lives of meaninglessness.
Paperback: 978-1-78535-699-5 ebook: 978-1-78535-700-8

In the Dust of This Planet
Horror of Philosophy vol. 1
Eugene Thacker
In the first of a series of three books on the Horror of Philosophy, *In the Dust of This Planet* offers the genre of horror as a way of thinking about the unthinkable.
Paperback: 978-1-84694-676-9 ebook: 978-1-78099-010-1

The End of Oulipo?
An Attempt to Exhaust a Movement
Lauren Elkin, Veronica Esposito
Paperback: 978-1-78099-655-4 ebook: 978-1-78099-656-1

Capitalist Realism
Is There No Alternative?
Mark Fisher
An analysis of the ways in which capitalism has presented itself
as the only realistic political-economic system.
Paperback: 978-1-84694-317-1 ebook: 978-1-78099-734-6

Rebel Rebel
Chris O'Leary
David Bowie: every single song. Everything you want to know,
everything you didn't know.
Paperback: 978-1-78099-244-0 ebook: 978-1-78099-713-1

Kill All Normies
Angela Nagle
Online culture wars from 4chan and Tumblr to Trump.
Paperback: 978-1- 78535-543-1 ebook: 978-1-78535-544-8

Cartographies of the Absolute
Alberto Toscano, Jeff Kinkle
An aesthetics of the economy for the twenty-first century.
Paperback: 978-1-78099-275-4 ebook: 978-1-78279-973-3

Babbling Corpse
Vaporwave and the Commodification of Ghosts
Grafton Tanner
Paperback: 978-1-78279-759-3 ebook: 978-1-78279-760-9

New Work New Culture
Work we want and a culture that strengthens us
Frithjoff Bergmann
A serious alternative for mankind and the planet.
Paperback: 978-1-78904-064-7 ebook: 978-1-78904-065-4

Malign Velocities

Accelerationism and Capitalism

Benjamin Noys

Long listed for the Bread and Roses Prize 2015, *Malign Velocities*
argues against the need for speed, tracking acceleration
as the symptom of the ongoing crises of capitalism.
Paperback: 978-1-78279-300-7 ebook: 978-1-78279-299-4

Meat Market

Female Flesh under Capitalism

Laurie Penny

A feminist dissection of women's bodies as the fleshy fulcrum of
capitalist cannibalism, whereby women are both consumers and
consumed.
Paperback: 978-1-84694-521-2 ebook: 978-1-84694-782-7

Romeo and Juliet in Palestine

Teaching Under Occupation

Tom Sperlinger

Life in the West Bank, the nature of pedagogy and the role of a
university under occupation.
Paperback: 978-1-78279-637-4 ebook: 978-1-78279-636-7

Ghosts of My Life

Writings on Depression, Hauntology and Lost Futures

Mark Fisher

Paperback: 978-1-78099-226-6 ebook: 978-1-78279-624-4

Why Are We The Good Guys?

Reclaiming your Mind from the Delusions of Propaganda

David Cromwell

A provocative challenge to the standard ideology that Western
power is a benevolent force in the world.
Paperback: 978-1-78099-365-2 ebook: 978-1-78099-366-9

Sweetening the Pill
or How We Got Hooked on Hormonal Birth Control
Holly Grigg-Spall
Has contraception liberated or oppressed women?
Sweetening the Pill breaks the silence on the dark side of hormonal
contraception.
Paperback: 978-1-78099-607-3 ebook: 978-1-78099-608-0

The Writing on the Wall
On the Decomposition of Capitalism and its Critics
Anselm Jappe, Alastair Hemmens
A new approach to the meaning of social emancipation.
Paperback: 978-1-78535-581-3 ebook: 978-1-78535-582-0

How to Dismantle the NHS in 10 Easy Steps (Second Edition)
Youssef El-Gingihy
The story of how your NHS was sold off and why you will have
to buy private health insurance soon. A new expanded second
edition with chapters on junior doctors' strikes and government
blueprints for US-style healthcare.
Paperback: 978-1-78904-178-1 ebook: 978-1-78904-179-8

Most titles are published in paperback and as an ebook.
Paperbacks are available in traditional bookshops. Both print and
ebook formats are available online.
Follow us on Facebook
at https://www.facebook.com/ZeroBooks
and Twitter at https://twitter.com/Zer0Books